A
LITERARY
HISTORY
OF
SPAIN

A LITERARY HISTORY OF SPAIN

General Editor: R. O. JONES
Cervantes Professor of Spanish, King's College, University of London

THE MIDDLE AGES
by A. D. DEYERMOND
Professor of Spanish, Westfield College, University of London

THE GOLDEN AGE: PROSE AND POETRY
by R. O. JONES

THE GOLDEN AGE: DRAMA
by EDWARD M. WILSON
Professor of Spanish, University of Cambridge
and DUNCAN MOIR
Lecturer in Spanish, University of Southampton

THE EIGHTEENTH CENTURY
by NIGEL GLENDINNING
Professor of Spanish, Trinity College, University of Dublin

THE NINETEENTH CENTURY
by DONALD L. SHAW
Senior Lecturer in Hispanic Studies, University of Edinburgh

THE TWENTIETH CENTURY
by G. G. BROWN
Lecturer in Spanish, Queen Mary College, University of London

SPANISH AMERICAN LITERATURE SINCE INDEPENDENCE
by JEAN FRANCO
Professor of Latin American Literature, University of Essex

CATALAN LITERATURE
by ARTHUR TERRY
Professor of Spanish, The Queen's University, Belfast

A LITERARY HISTORY OF SPAIN

CATALAN LITERATURE

A LITERARY
HISTORY OF SPAIN

CATALAN LITERATURE

ARTHUR TERRY

Professor of Spanish
The Queen's University, Belfast

LONDON · ERNEST BENN LIMITED

NEW YORK · BARNES & NOBLE BOOKS

First published 1972 by Ernest Benn Limited
25 New Street Square, Fleet Street, London EC4A 3JA
and Harper & Row Publishers Inc.
Barnes & Noble Import Division
10 East 33rd Street, New York 10022

Distributed in Canada by
The General Publishing Company Limited, Toronto

© Arthur Terry 1972

Printed in Great Britain

ISBN 0 510-32299-9

ISBN 0 06-4968103 (USA)

Paperback 0 510-32300-6

Paperback 0 06-4968111 (USA)

For

JOAN and ELIZABETH GILI

CONTENTS

FOREWORD BY THE GENERAL EDITOR

SPANISH, the language of what was in its day the greatest of European powers, became the common tongue of the most far-flung Empire the world had until then seen. Today, in number of speakers, Spanish is one of the world's major languages. The literature written in Spanish is correspondingly rich. The earliest European lyrics in a post-classical vernacular that we know of (if we except Welsh and Irish) were written in Spain; the modern novel was born there; there too was written some of the greatest European poetry and drama; and some of the most interesting works of our time are being written in Spanish.

Nevertheless, this new history may require some explanation and even justification. Our justification is that a new and up-to-date English-language history seemed called for to serve the increasing interest now being taken in Spanish. There have been other English-language histories in the past, some of them very good, but none on this scale.

Every history is a compromise between aims difficult or even impossible to reconcile. This one is no exception. While imaginative literature is our main concern, we have tried to relate that literature to the society in and for which it was written, but without sub-ordinating criticism to amateur sociology. Since not everything could be given equal attention (even if it were desirable to do so) we have concentrated on those writers and works of manifestly outstanding artistic importance to us their modern readers, with the inevitable consequence that many interesting minor writers are reduced to names and dates, and the even lesser are often not mentioned at all. Though we have tried also to provide a usable work of general reference, we offer the history primarily as a guide to the understanding and appreciation of what we consider of greatest value in the literatures of Spain and Spanish America.

Beyond a necessary minimum, no attempt has been made to arrive at uniform criteria; the history displays therefore the variety of approach and opinion that is to be found in a good university department of literature, a variety which we hope will prove stimulating. Each section takes account of the accepted works of scholarship in its field, but we do not offer our history as a grey consensus of received opinions; each contributor has imposed his own interpretation to the extent that this could be supported with solid scholarship and argument.

Though the literature of Spanish America is not to be regarded simply as an offshoot of the literature of Spain, it seemed natural to link the two in our history since Spanish civilisation has left an indelible stamp on the Americas. Since Catalonia has been so long a part of Spain it seemed equally justified to include Catalan literature, an important influence on Spanish literature at certain times, and a highly interesting literature in its own right.

The bibliographies are not meant to be exhaustive. They are intended only as a guide to further reading. For more exhaustive inquiry recourse should be had to general bibliographies such as that by J. Simón Díaz.

R.O.J.

PREFACE

In writing this brief history of Catalan literature, I have tried to bear in mind the needs of the non-specialist reader with some knowledge of Spanish who wishes to know more about an important but, on the whole, neglected area of Peninsular culture. Where English readers are concerned, the task, unfortunately, is long overdue: in a recent and otherwise excellent literary encyclopedia, the whole of Catalan literature is allotted the same amount of space as Jean-Paul Sartre, and this seems characteristic of a situation which few specialists as yet have tried to alter. The chief barrier, of course, is linguistic: yet it is not difficult to acquire at least a reading knowledge of Catalan, and for reasons which are given in Chapter I, the older literature is relatively accessible to a modern reader compared, say, with that of France or Spain.

This accessibility gives an impression of coherence to the entire range of Catalan literature which is reinforced to a great extent by social and historical tendencies. Roughly speaking, Catalan literature follows a recognisable European pattern, with one notable exception: the fact that its course is interrupted for something like three centuries by what is usually known as the period of 'Decadence' (see Chapter 2). To see why this should be so demands an awareness of certain historical facts, and these in turn point to the close interpenetration of literature and society which is evident in most phases of Catalan culture. Both the nineteenth-century revival and the more conscious programmes of *noucentisme* in the twentieth are attempts to create a new national identity, a task which has lost none of its urgency in the years since the Spanish Civil War. At various stages in Catalan history, this sense of identity has existed within the context of some larger political unit: Carolingian France, Aragon, Spain. This makes for many of the tensions and difficulties which still beset Catalan writers and which give the best contemporary literature its most characteristic flavour. At the same time, an impartial observer cannot fail to be struck by the very distinctive nature of Catalan society compared with the rest of the Peninsula, and by the obvious European quality which goes with the best features of this society and its literature. In the last half-century, an impressive number of Catalan painters, architects, and musicians—Miró, Dalí, Tàpies, Gaudí, Roberto Gerhard, Pau Casals, Montserrat Caballé—have been acclaimed outside their own country. What is not generally realised is that all of these share a common cultural heritage and that their achievement in the non-verbal arts is matched by a similar degree of excellence in literature. As I have tried to show, modern Catalan writers are just as much concerned with their relations to earlier traditions as their contemporaries in other countries, and their solutions are often suggestive outside their own immediate literary context.

Needless to say, a book like this makes no claims to exhaustiveness. Since information on Catalan writers is generally lacking in English, it seemed best to give as much space as possible to major authors and tendencies, and to exclude those minor writers whose interest is mainly documentary. At the same time, I hope that something of the general social background has emerged, and I have tried in the opening section to touch briefly on certain basic facts of language which directly affect the growth of literary expression. I have also added literal translations of the passages quoted in Catalan. In order to keep the bibliography within manageable limits, I have only listed basic editions of literary texts, though a good many works of criticism are referred to in the notes. In this, as in the rest of the book, my chief aim has been to provide the reader with a clear and, as far as possible, accurate introduction to a literature which I hope he will be encouraged to explore for himself.

A.T.

Belfast,
June 1971

LIST OF ABBREVIATIONS

AC	*Antologia Catalana*
BHS	*Bulletin of Hispanic Studies*
ENC	*Els nostres clàssics*
ER	*Estudis Romànics* (Barcelona)
HR	*Hispanic Review*
MLR	*Modern Language Review*
SdO	*Serra d'Or* (Barcelona)

Chapter 1

MEDIEVAL AND EARLY RENAISSANCE

I. LANGUAGE AND HISTORY

THE ORIGINS OF CATALAN LITERATURE, like those of any other, depend very largely on the interplay of language and history. Of the Romance languages, Catalan is one of those, like Provençal and Portuguese, which have remained closest to their Latin roots. As might be expected from its geographical distribution, it forms a bridge-language between the Ibero-Romance and Gallo-Romance groups, sharing in both, but never completely absorbed by either. Two facts stand out from pre-Roman times: the existence of an ethnic division, running south-south-east from the central Pyrenees, which affected the later dialect division between eastern and western Catalan; and, conversely, an early ethnic and cultural link between north-east Catalonia and the South of France which remained unbroken until the middle of the thirteenth century. Thus, when the Catalan language began to take on a separate identity in the course of the eleventh century, the old Roman division of Septimania, with its centre at Béziers, was still united politically with the Tarraconensis, the north-east province of Spain, while ecclesiastically the whole area was controlled by the archbishop of Narbonne. From a linguistic point of view, this meant that Catalan, which might have become another language of the Ibero-Romance group, was pulled in the direction of Gallo-Romance at the most crucial period in its formation.

The political origins of Catalonia add another dimension. A little before A.D. 800, less than a century after the Moorish invasion, the country was reconquered by the Franks and

I

divided into counties; later, in 864, these were regrouped to form the *Marca Hispanica*, conceived as a Carolingian buffer-state between France and Moorish-occupied Spain. By 900, the Frankish influence was beginning to weaken, and a strong Catalan dynasty had established itself in the north-east of the Peninsula, with its focus in Barcelona. The effect of the Frankish connection, however, continued to make itself felt in other ways: as a result, Catalonia and the south of France developed a more comprehensive feudal system than the rest of Spain, and the links between the newly founded monasteries on either side of the Pyrenees helped to establish Ripoll, the traditional mausoleum of the counts of Barcelona, as an international centre of learning in the eleventh century. On the other hand, the early centuries of the Reconquest did very little to strengthen relations between Catalonia and the rest of the Peninsula, and by the time Catalan interests moved beyond the Ebro, in the second half of the twelfth century, it was too late for the basic features of the language to be affected.

Between 900 and 1300, the Catalan language developed fairly quickly; any later changes were minor and more gradual.[1] This rapid evolution of the language coincided with a period of territorial expansion. In 1137, the Houses of Barcelona and Aragon were united by the marriage of Ramon Berenguer IV to the Aragonese heiress, Petronila, an event which had the effect of postponing the union of Aragon and Castile for several centuries. Early in the thirteenth century, relations with the south of France suffered a permanent setback when Pere I[2] was killed at the battle of Muret (1213), fighting in support of the Albigensians against the army of Simon de Montfort.[3] By this defeat, Catalan rights north of the Pyrenees were restricted to Roussillon and Montpellier, a situation which was confirmed by Pere's successor, Jaume I, in the Treaty of Corbeil (1258). In the same reign, however, Catalan ambitions turned in two new directions. It was at this stage that Catalan expansion in the Mediterranean began, with the conquest of Mallorca (1229), followed closely by that of the other Balearic Islands: the first phase of a movement which was eventually to spread to Corsica, Sardinia, Naples, and the Aegean. And almost simultaneously, with the conquest of Valencia (1238) and the settlement of the lands to the south, the modern limits of the Catalan-speaking area were practically filled out, with Valencian and *mallorquí* as its two most important dialects.

Literary Catalan remains extraordinarily unified throughout the Middle Ages. The main reason for this, apart from the relatively static nature of the language itself, is the standardising influence of the Royal Chancellory of Aragon. Dialect usages, except for occasional Valencianisms, only appear to any extent after 1500, that is to say, in the period of literary decline which follows the break-up of the Catalan Court.

Compared with French or Spanish, Catalan is more faithful to Latin, and consequently more archaic in appearance, even at the present day. Anyone hearing the language for the first time will be struck by its consonantal quality; in W. J. Entwistle's phrase, 'Catalan is more abrupt than Spanish'.[4] There are two main reasons for this: the loss of post-tonic vowels other than *a* (*e* is occasionally found as a support-vowel, e.g. PATREM 〉 *pare*), and the absence of the spontaneous diphthongisation which is such a feature of Spanish (e.g. CAELUM 〉 Sp. *cielo*, but Cat. *cel*).[5] The first of these tendencies means that Catalan has a much higher proportion of final consonants than Spanish or Portuguese.[6] This gives a distinctive rhythm to the language, which is particularly noticeable in verse. Thus, the opening lines of a famous poem by Ausias March (see below, pp. 39-45),

> Qui no és trist, de mos dictats no cur,
> o en algun temps que sia trist estat,[7]

appear in the Spanish translation of Jorge de Montemayor (1560) as

> No cure de mis versos, ni los lea
> quien no fuese muy triste, o lo haya sido.

It is such facts of language which give a piece of prose or verse its distinctive sound and weight. Compared with other varieties of Romance, there is a quality of roughness in the Catalan language, even at its most sophisticated. It would be wrong, of course, to regard this as something primitive or undeveloped. The best Catalan writers of any period seem to treat it, however unconsciously, as a source of vitality; conversely, one is made to feel that any attempt to eliminate these rougher sounds could only weaken the literary language.

II. THE CATALAN TROUBADOURS

It may seem strange to begin a history of Catalan literature with an account of poetry in Provençal. One needs to remember, however, that no other vernacular literature existed in Catalonia before the 1260s, and that the close similarity between Catalan and Provençal at this stage was accentuated by the deliberately restricted idiom of troubadour poetry. More important still, one can point to the continuity of a tradition which remained virtually unchallenged until the fifteenth century. Though later poets often wrote a very defective kind of Provençal, they clearly had no intention of using their own language; on the other hand, Ausias March (1397-1459), the first major poet to write in Catalan, cannot be fully understood without a knowledge of the earlier tradition, to which he bears a strong, if oblique, relationship.

In terms of quantity, the Catalan contribution to the body of troubadour poetry is quite small: 197 poems, out of a total of more than 2,500. Yet, of the twenty-four poets whose names are known, several are highly gifted, and at least one, Cerverí de Girona, is among the major exponents of the tradition. Their work spans roughly a century and a quarter, from about 1160 to 1290, though the most active period comes in the reigns of Alfons I (1162-96) and Pere I (1196-1213). During these years, many of the most famous Provençal troubadours visited the Catalan Court; both kings were amateur poets themselves, and

Alfons is known to have taken part in a poetic debate with Giraut de Bornelh. It is clear, moreover, that such relations were not merely literary: like other rulers of the time, the kings of Aragon realised the political advantages of encouraging the troubadours, whose repertoire included topical and satirical forms like the *sirventes*, useful both for political propaganda and for ridiculing one's enemies.

After 1213, the centre of gravity of the troubadour tradition shifts south of the Pyrenees. From now on, poets tend to move about less, and when they do, it is usually in the direction of the Court of Toledo. There is also a noticeable change in social status: where the earlier Catalan troubadours, like Guillem de Bergadà, were often feudal lords whose poetry carried the weight of political authority, in the thirteenth century there is a blurring of categories between the troubadours and the minstrels or *joglars*. The distinction, in fact, had never been a very firm one: in theory, the troubadour was an original poet and the *joglar* a performer or reciter of other people's verse, yet there are various instances of minstrels, like Ramon Vidal de Besalú, who were poets as well. As far as Catalonia is concerned, the activities of the *joglars* are on the whole poorly documented, though there are signs that here, as in other countries, they were reciters of epic and narrative poetry. What these poems were, or in which language they were performed, one can only guess, though it seems clear that the chief epic cycles, in one form or another, were known in Catalonia by the second half of the twelfth century, possibly in Provençal versions, and that a native Catalan epic poetry, now lost in its original form, must have survived long enough to serve as a source for the prose chronicles of Desclot and Muntaner (see below, pp. 26-9).[8] As for the thirteenth century, it appears that, while the number of poets of noble origin declined, the demand for *joglars* increased, and, though the latter were still regarded chiefly as entertainers, those who were also original poets, like Cerverí de Girona, occasionally achieved great fame at Court.

One general impression emerges from the poetry of the time:

that the greatest successes of the Catalan troubadours almost invariably lie outside the sphere of the courtly love-poem which is
usually taken to be the central achievement of the tradition.
Nearly all of them make use at times of the commonplaces of
troubadour love-poetry, and several, like Guillem de Cabestany
(*c.* 1175-*post* 1212), achieve a certain distinction within their
limited range. The most memorable poems of this period, however, are what Peter Dronke has called 'lyrics of realism',[9] meaning by this a kind of poem which, though not necessarily truthful
in an autobiographical sense, either refers to real events or chooses
to disregard conventional attitudes in favour of personal authenticity.

Three examples may help to make this clear. The first is
Guillem de Bergadà (late twelfth century), probably the best
instance of a poet who, though he writes in Provençal, has very
little to do with the courtly love tradition. As a feudal lord continually at odds with other nobles, and at times with the king
himself, it is hardly surprising that he should excel in satire and
invective. Certainly, his poetry is full of unflattering allusions to
his contemporaries, and he uses irony and ridicule with deadly
effect. Or, as his early Provençal biographer puts it: 'he composed good *sirventes* in which he spoke ill of some and good of
others, and used to boast that every lady was in love with him'.

Yet on the few occasions when he composes a serious love-
poem, he achieves a degree of refinement which can command
the respect of Arnaut Daniel, perhaps the most fastidious of all
his contemporaries. This ambivalence is characteristic of both the
man and the poet. For a time in the 1180s, Guillem appears as
the respected companion of Bertran de Born and Richard Coeur
de Lion, then duke of Aquitaine, and there are witnesses to his
striking presence in the various Catalan Courts; nevertheless,
there are signs that he was ill at ease among his own kind and
that his real sympathies probably lay with the less reputable
society of the *joglars*. This may account for one of the peculiar
strengths of his poetry: its ability to draw on the melodies and
rhythms of popular verse which has since disappeared, as in the

refrain of the poem which begins 'Cantarey mentre m'estau' ('I shall sing while I am at leisure'):

> Puys van xantan liridumvau,
> balan, notan gent e suau...
> puys van xantan liridumvar,
> balan, notan autet e clar.[10]

This snatch of a children's song is all the more striking since it runs through a poem in which Guillem mercilessly attacks some of his worst enemies. Significantly, his one really moving poem, the *Planh*, or lament, for Ponç de Mataplana, comes from a similar clash of feeling. Some time after 1180, Ponç de Mataplana, a man who is constantly vilified in his earlier poems, died fighting against the Moors. In the opening lines of the *Planh*, all the former hatred is retracted: the one-time enemy is praised for his bravery and generosity, and the poet wishes he could have fought beside him in his last battle. The sincerity of this is unquestionable, and the whole poem goes far beyond the range of the conventional lament. At the same time, there are moments when Guillem hints at the procedure laid down for such poems in the troubadour manuals of rhetoric, and particularly at certain religious *topoi*. The result, however, like the lament as a whole, is strikingly individual. Instead of the usual closing invocation to God or the Virgin, the poem ends with the vision of a curiously worldly paradise:

> E paradis el luoc melhor,
> lai o.l bon rei de Fransa es,
> prop de Rolan, sai que l'arm'es
> de Mon Marques de Mataplana;
> e mon joglar de Ripoles,
> e mon Sabata eisamens,
> estan ab las domnas gensors
> sobre'u pali cobert de flors,
> josta N'Olivier de Lausana.[11]

The second example is a single poem, the verse dialogue by

Ramon Vidal de Besalú which begins 'Abrils iss'e mays intrava' ('April was departing and May was coming in'). Ramon Vidal seems to stand at the point of transition between two distinct phases of troubadour poetry. In this poem, written possibly in 1212, the difference can be seen in the attitudes of the two speakers, the author himself and the young *joglar* with whom he discusses the aims and status of courtly poetry. The younger man complains of the decline in the quality of patronage which has taken place since the time of Alfons I; the more experienced poet accepts this, but appears to regard humiliation and lack of esteem as normal professional risks. There is no sense here, as there is later in Cerverí de Girona, that poetic skill is its own justification: everything still depends on the attitude of a discriminating audience, even if this has become harder to find.

It is perhaps significant that Ramon Vidal's best-known poem, the *Castia gilós*, or 'Warning to the jealous', looks back nostalgically at the Court of Alfonso VIII of Castile (1170-1214). This fable of a jealous husband, set in a courtly framework and told with a sure sense of irony, suggests an easy kind of relationship between poet and audience which becomes much rarer as the century advances. Nevertheless, it would be wrong to regard Ramon Vidal as a backward-looking poet. If his main concern is to find the best way of pleasing his public, he has a sense of the universal appeal of poetry which goes beyond the courtly milieu. Like Guillem de Bergadà, he is aware of folk culture, and in his prose treatise on the art of poetry, *Las rasos de trobar*, he writes: 'There is scarcely a place, however remote or solitary ... where you will not immediately hear singing ... for the greatest pleasure men have—even the shepherds on the mountains—is to sing'.

Thirdly, there is Cerverí de Girona (also known as Guillem de Cervera), the last and greatest of the Catalan troubadours, whose poems were written between 1250 and 1280. Strictly speaking, Cerverí is not a troubadour, but a *joglar* who succeeded in establishing himself as a professional poet, first at the Court of Jaume I, and eventually in the service of the latter's son, the future Pere II (1276-85). The 120 or so poems of his which have survived show an astonishing variety of tones, from the popular lyric to the rhetorical ingenuities of *trobar clus*. Most of his love-poems fall into the second category, and form the least interesting part of his work. What impresses one in his better poems, apart from their strong moral overtones, is the combination of humour, commonsense, and fluency. Once again, Cerverí is a poet who is able to draw on unsophisticated modes. One such lyric, the *viadeyra* which begins 'No. 1 prenatz lo fals marit,/Jana delgada',[12] is quite clearly a *chanson de mal mariée* of a type familiar in other literatures, though it is unlike any other Provençal poem of the period. The name *viadeyra* or *viandela* suggests a kind of poem which is improvised on a journey; it is referred to in the contemporary manuals of rhetoric as 'the lowest kind of song', a sure sign that it belongs to a popular tradition. The most surprising feature is the actual form of the verse: the use of parallelism and refrain reminiscent of the Galician–Portuguese lyric, a type of poetry which Cerverí must certainly have been aware of, since he is known to have visited the Court of Alfonso X of Castile in 1269. Beyond this, one can only speculate, though it is not unlikely, as Riquer suggests (1, 132), that the example of established poets who were not above making use of a different kind of popular tradition may have persuaded Cerverí to look more seriously at the possibilities of Catalan folk-song.

On the surface, the type of moral reflection which runs through much of Cerverí's verse sounds very like the observations one finds in the didactic poems of Ramon Vidal: a resigned pessimism in the face of a world which is not all that it should be. But if one compares these generalisations with the more detailed reflections on the status of the poet and his art, an important difference begins to emerge. Like Ramon Vidal, Cerverí is very conscious of his standing as a professional poet, but his general attitude is much less passive. In many of his poems, the use of the second person, *tu* and *vos*, is almost obsessive, as if he wished at all costs to establish a personal relationship with his audience. Few other poets of the time are as intimate as this, or as concerned to impress their moral independence on the hearer. Few, either, are so conscious of style or, as he himself puts it, of the need to achieve subtlety of expression without loss of clarity. What is really original in Cerverí, however, is the way in which all these considerations are woven into his conception of the artist. His complaints against the indignities which a professional poet is made to suffer by his masters are more specific than those of Ramon Vidal. As he says in a poem addressed to another *joglar*:

> Minten dizetz als rics lauzengeria,
> minten prendetz qu'esters hom no.us daria,
> minten chantatz e comtatz ab falsia;
> mintetz per gaug e mintetz ab feunia ...
> qu'entratz manjar ses cost on que sia,
> e par siatz repentit d' eretgia
> que sols manjatz ses tota compaynia.[13]

Sometimes he rejects the name of *joglar*; at other times he resigns himself to it, but reminds his audience that in the past the same profession has included kings and saints:

> Si motz laçan trobars es juglaria,
> eu e.l rey aut n'em juglar d'una guia.[14]

What sustains him, ultimately, is a sense of his own worth and a satisfaction in literary excellence for its own sake. And the sanction for this comes, not from any audience, but from nature itself:

> Dels lays dels auzelos
> c'ay auzits en la prada
> ay ma lengua afilada.[15]

In one of his most memorable poems, Cerverí is asked why he is reluctant to recite his poems in public. His answer is that a beautiful lady keeps them under lock and key; in this way, she is made to say, 'pus jo esmer e aprim ton saber'.[16] The allegory is finely conceived: the lady represents the desire for perfection, and the longer she keeps the poems concealed from the public the more subtle will the poet's skill become.

Such confidence in the poet's own powers, like the high conception of poetry it implies, is unique in medieval Catalan literature. Though courtly patronage continues to function, in one form or another, until the end of the Middle Ages, the whole poetic tradition declines sharply early in the fourteenth century, and already in the lifetime of Cerverí de Girona the literary scene is changing dramatically with the appearance of the first vernacular prose. Cerverí, the last major poet of the classical troubadour tradition, died soon after 1282. This is the point, one feels, at which Catalan might have replaced Provençal as the language of serious poetry. Nevertheless, Ramon Llull (1233-1316), the first great master of Catalan prose, continued to write his own poems in Provençal, even though their content is very different from that of troubadour poetry. No doubt the linguistic situation seemed much less clear-cut at the time, yet there is one contemporary witness who, perhaps because he was writing at some distance from the centre of literary activity, shows signs of having grasped what was happening. This is Jofre de Foixà, a Benedictine monk and a minor troubadour at the Sicilian Court. His grammatical treatise, the *Regles de trobar* (1289-91), was written at the command of the king of Sicily, soon to become Jaume II of Aragon. Though it was intended as a complement to the *Rasos de trobar* of Ramon Vidal de Besalú (see above, p. 8), the differences are very striking. For one thing, Jofre de Foixà is much more conscious of linguistic differences: not only does he define the territorial extension of Provençal with considerable accuracy, but he asserts that French and Catalan are distinct languages, which must not be confused with Provençal. Though basically he is arguing for the purity of poetic language, he does so in terms which could hardly have occurred to Ramon Vidal. In the intervening period, two things have taken place: the original cultural unity of Catalonia and the south of France has been weakened, and the Catalan language has emerged as a serious prose medium. Much of his detailed discussion of grammatical usage depends on a clear awareness of the differences between Catalan and Provençal. At one point, however, he goes further and states an important general principle:

> I admit that, in terms of art, he [i.e. Ramon Vidal] spoke the truth, and that such words should be written as he says; but I do not agree that the troubadours were wrong, for usage overrules art, and an established custom is held lawful when it imposes itself through usage.

'Art' here means grammar and 'usage' the language of everyday speech. Comparing this distinction with the earlier one between Provençal and Catalan, a simple but crucial idea emerges: if grammar is based on fixed rules, Provençal is also a 'fixed' poetic medium in the sense that it deliberately excludes all dialect variations; 'usage', on the other hand, constantly changes, just as it is Catalan which is the naturally developing language of speech and written prose.

III. RAMON LLULL; ARNAU DE VILANOVA

Ramon Llull (1233-1316) is not only the creator of Catalan literary prose, but also one of the most remarkable men of his time. The first thirty years of his life gave no indication of what was to follow: he was born in Mallorca, of noble parents; in his twenties, he became tutor and steward to the future Jaume II and, while at Court, he married and had children. In his most remarkable poem, *Lo Desconhort*, written in old age, he remembers his early years: his life as a courtier had, by his own account, been ostentatious and dissolute, and in the course of it he had written a certain amount of troubadour verse, none of which has survived. Some time between 1262 and 1265, all this changed: as the result of a repeated vision of Christ on the Cross, Llull underwent what is usually referred to as his 'conversion'. This was the beginning of a period of intense spiritual activity and copious writing which lasted until his death. After pilgrimages to Compostela, Rome, and Jerusalem, he devoted himself to religious studies, and by 1275 is known to have written sixteen books, including one of his major works, the *Libre de contemplació*. By the end of his life, this number had increased to 243; in the meantime, he had founded the monastery of Miramar (Mallorca) as a centre for the teaching of oriental languages, had preached in North Africa and defended his ideas at the Sorbonne, and had crossed and re-crossed the south of Europe many times, expounding his plans for the renewal of Christendom before kings, popes, and councils of the Church. These plans entailed three simple but demanding aims: the conversion of non-Christians, the correction of theo-logical errors (particularly those of the Averroists) through books and public controversy, and the training of missionaries for work in North Africa and the Middle East.

Though the energy which Llull devoted to these projects was unique, the directions they took clearly owed a great deal to contemporary circumstances. The crusading ideal which deter-mined so many of his actions was still generally felt in western Europe, and must have been all the more real for Llull by the fact of living in Mallorca, a recently conquered territory which still retained a large Muslim community. Moreover, his project for an *Ars magna* belongs to the general revival of the theology and legal theory which culminated in the *Summa* of his slightly older contemporary, St Thomas Aquinas (*c.* 1227-74), just as his strong bias towards teaching and writing in the vernacular seems to reflect the whole background of late thirteenth-century popu-lar devotion. One must be careful, however, not to draw the links too close. Llull's independence of mind is present in almost everything he wrote: though his ideas are indebted to the teach-ing of several religious orders, he seems never to have identified himself completely with any one, and, unlike his contemporary Arnau de Vilanova (see below, p. 23), he remained indifferent, if not actually hostile, to the popular movements of the time.

Catalan prose before Llull consisted entirely of translations: legal texts, chronicles, and parts of the Bible. Llull's special distinction lies in having been not only the creator of philosophical and theological writing in Catalan, but also of imaginative prose. Though he also used Latin and Arabic on occasion, it is his presence as a philosopher–poet of genius at the beginning of the vernacular tradition which is of incalculable significance for the later history of literary Catalan. The normative value of his work is clear from the extent to which its diffusion helped to create the linguistic standards which were later to be maintained by the Royal Chancellory. Llull himself had no illusions about the difficulty of achieving such a norm. In the *Libre de contemplació* (*c.* 1272), he complains of the inadequacy of words to express the subtleties of the mind:

> Car moltes vegades s'esdevé que enteniment entén una cosa, e paraula ne significa altra contrària a la veritat que l'enteniment entén ...[17]

His attempt to overcome this limitation through the use of similitudes (*semblances*) which speak to the imagination is central to his literary technique. A similitude for Llull can mean anything from an aphorism to a complete fable. The technique is basically that of the popular preacher, though Llull's use of it can be extremely subtle; as he himself recognised, obscurity itself can serve a useful purpose in stretching the mind of the reader: 'Car on pus escura és la semblança, pus altament entén l'enteniment qui aquella semblança entén'.[18]

Another part of Llull's rhetorical theory—his insistence that the aesthetic value of words depends entirely on the intrinsic value of the objects or creatures they signify—may seem strange to a modern reader. Yet if 'angel' and 'king', as he argues, are nobler words than 'knight' or 'peasant', this follows naturally from the medieval notion of a hierarchical universe which Llull takes as the basis of his own speculations. It is important to realise that there is no clear dividing-line between his more literary writing and the rest: his entire work is an attempt to relate the nature of the created universe to that of God Himself, and in basing his arguments on the accepted world picture he knew that he was working with elements common to the

Christian, Jewish, and Muslim traditions—a fact which was of enormous importance for his missionary aims.

No brief account can convey either the imaginative sweep or the mathematical coherence of Llull's vision of creation.[19] One of his many proverbs sets the tone for his whole endeavour: 'Puja ton entendre e pujaràs ton amor'.[20] The idea that man's ultimate justification lies in his love of God is common to many religious writers; what distinguishes Llull is the importance he attaches to the role of the understanding. This, in turn, accounts for the expository nature of so much of his work, the extent to which he feels bound to explain and illustrate every detail of his complex system of truths. Exposition, in Llull's sense, often goes beyond rational discourse: at times he needs to speak through metaphor and fable because words themselves are insufficient. In practice, his attempts to convince his readers take many forms; what varies most is his technique of persuasion, the types of strategy which determine the angle of approach in individual works. From a literary point of view, Llull's most memorable effects are achieved through allegory and symbol: the tree of life in *L'arbre de ciència*, the prison of love in the *Arbre de filosofia d'amor*, and the mysterious forest through which the hero of the *Blanquerna* moves on his spiritual quest. Allegory for Llull is not only a means of giving imaginative force to his ideas, but a way of drawing together an encyclopaedic mass of detail in a final overarching synthesis.

Llull's immense skill in controlling a complex pattern of events and reflections is demonstrated very clearly in his two prose narratives, the *Blanquerna*, or *Romanç d'Evast e Blanquerna*, and the *Libre de Fèlix*, also known as the *Libre de Meravelles*. If one hesitates to describe these books as novels, it is only because they contain an unusually high proportion of expository and other non-fictional material. In view of Llull's actual intentions, however, this is scarcely a fault. Like the rest of his work, both these books are primarily didactic; the fact that for once Llull was willing to explore the resources of contemporary verse narrative (notably the *roman* and the *fabliau*) merely shows his wish to enlarge his audience by working in more popular genres.

Of the two works, the *Blanquerna* is the more perfectly achieved. Its structure is impressively simple. Each of its five books corresponds to a particular mode of existence: the first describes the married life of Blanquerna's parents, Evast and Aloma, together with his own birth and upbringing; subsequently, Blanquerna becomes in turn a monk, an abbot, and a bishop, is elected pope, and finally achieves his original intention of living as a hermit. In this last state, he composes the *Libre d'Amic e Amat*, the finest of Llull's mystical writings, and the *Art de contemplació*, a short treatise on the art of meditation.

Technically, the *Blanquerna* shows a number of features which look forward to later and more celebrated works of fiction. The plot itself both advances through time and returns on itself in a cyclical pattern: in the central part of the action, we see how Blanquerna's sense of vocation is frustrated, though his experience is enriched as a result. More strikingly, Llull projects himself into the story at several points through the figure of 'Ramon lo foll', a former nobleman now deranged by the love of God, who has come to Rome in order to expose the vices of the Papal Court. Finally, in both the *Blanquerna* and the *Fèlix*, Llull uses the device of the 'book within a book': in the epilogue to his story, Blanquerna is reading the *Libre de contemplació* (one of Llull's earlier works) when he is interrupted by a minstrel who has repented of the evils of his profession; as a penance, Blanquerna orders him to spread good through the world by reading publicly from 'The romance of Evast and Blanquerna'.

What makes the *Blanquerna* a masterpiece, however, is the depth and range of human experience which it conveys. The major decisions which the hero is compelled to make are hardly ever simple choices between right and wrong. Though we are convinced that it is spiritually necessary for Blanquerna to leave home, and, in doing so, to disappoint his parents' ambitions for him, we are made to feel the emotional force of his mother's distress. In this and other episodes, the dramatic tension comes from the sense of moral rectitude which is present in each of the protagonists. Similarly, even when the interests of one party are morally flawed, as in Aloma's plans for Blanquerna's marriage, we are allowed to sympathise with the purely human aspect of the situation. Llull's greatest psychological achievement, however, is in the presentation of his hero. Blanquerna's spiritual quest, as the structure of the book makes clear, is a highly tortuous one, in which chance plays almost as great a part as conscious decision. This pattern is repeated in many of the individual episodes: Blanquerna is made credible precisely because he is prone to make mistakes and to experience temptation, and in the end this gives him an authority which other characters are obliged to recognise. In Chapter LII, for example, Blanquerna is riding through a forest with a young girl whom he has just rescued from the knight who had kidnapped her. Both are tempted to sin: Blanquerna resists, but the girl, in her gratitude, offers herself to him. Neither the author nor his hero makes any attempt to condemn her: she has merely revealed a human failing which Blanquerna himself has had to overcome. Blanquerna speaks to her unpretentiously of God and the power of prayer, and she accepts his words without hesitation:

> La donzella conec que Blanquerna li deia aquelles paraules per ço car havia conegut ço de què era temptada, e loà e beneí Déu, qui tanta de virtut havia donada a Blanquerna contra temptació.[21]

Though Blanquerna's quest takes him through forests and wildernesses, several parts of the book are densely populated. The social spectrum which Llull presents is as comprehensive as anything in medieval fiction, ranging from popes and emperors to the thieves and prostitutes of Rome. In a sense, this is another aspect of the novel's credibility: if Blanquerna's spiritual progress is to carry conviction, it must be shown as humanly possible within the terms of contemporary society. Sooner or later, however, the question of realism arises, of how far Llull is concerned with accurate social observation. On this point, modern critics are noticeably divided. To take one example: Blanquerna's father is a merchant who has married a woman of noble birth. In the opening chapters, both parents are concerned to give Blanquerna the kind of education which will enable him eventually to administer the family fortunes. Some critics have seen this as a deliberate attempt on Llull's part to emphasise the role of the new middle classes, a fact which, if it were true, would support the view that the novel is an essentially bourgeois genre. It is possible to argue, however, that they are forcing the evidence: that, in fact, the particular kind of humility which Llull ascribes to Evast only makes its full effect when his commercial activities are seen from an aristocratic point of view.

Here, and in other episodes, it is easy to exaggerate the 'social truth' of a situation by applying exclusively modern criteria. What is unquestionable is the degree of intimacy which Llull achieves in describing the married life of Evast and Aloma, and the extent to which he is prepared to suggest the quality and detail of everyday life. In Chapter XII, for instance, the pair of them, having sold their possessions in order to devote themselves to charity, are begging at the houses of two rich couples who have gone to Mass. It starts to rain, and, we are told:

> De cascún dels albergs eixí una serventa, qui portaven a l'esgleia capa de pluja e galotxes a son senyor e a sa dama.[22]

More impressively, in Chapter XIX, Natana, the girl whom Blanquerna has refused to marry, looks out of her window and sees in turn a bridal procession, a funeral, and a criminal being led to execution. Such telling details help to create an effect of social depth; for the most part, however, this is achieved by suggestion rather than by the steady accumulation of realistic observation. What realism there is in the novel tends to be limited and fragmentary. The main emphasis is on social concern, rather than on actual social observation, a bias which is particularly evident in the Third Book, which describes Blanquerna's career as a bishop. The formation of Blanquerna's social conscience, in fact, is a fundamental part of the book's message: the vision of a Christian utopia which does not reject existing society, but shows how faith and good actions can transform the most common human situations.

Blanquerna's double vision of society is suggested in the actual title of Llull's other fictional narrative, the *Fèlix*, or *Libre de meravelles*. In the context, the word *meravelles* is clearly ambiguous: not only does the hero marvel at the wonders of creation, he is also amazed and horrified at the extent of man's corruption. Compared with the *Blanquerna*, the *Fèlix* is more loosely knit, and its total impact less forceful. The narrative interest is thinner, and a large part of the book is modelled on the type of encyclopaedic dialogue between master and disciple common in medieval didactic literature. The most remarkable section, the *Libre de les bèsties*, was written earlier than the rest of the book and forms a completely independent narrative. In it, Llull uses the technique of the beast fable to write a bitter satire against corrupt kings and their courts. Though there are obvious debts to the *Calila e Dimna* and the *Roman de Renart*, Llull's manipulation of his sources is extremely skilful. In contrast to other examples of the genre, the *Libre de les bèsties* reverses the technique by which men are made to tell stories about the moral behaviour of animals, so that it is the animals who take their examples from human actions. Nor is it a satire against feudal society: it is clear from other works, like the *Libre de l'Orde de cavalleria*, that Llull completely accepted the hierarchical system of his time, and in the *Libre de les bèsties* there is a strong implication that the sense of honour is confined to the upper levels of society.

If the *Libre de les bèsties*, for all its artistry, is related only obliquely to Llull's major concerns, the *Libre d'Amic e Amat*, which forms part of the final book of the *Blanquerna*, is the finest of all Llull's spiritual writings and one of the greatest mystical texts of the Middle Ages. Because of this, it is a work which cannot be discussed in purely literary terms. Though it contains passages of great beauty—in some ways it is a far greater lyrical achievement than Llull's actual poetry—the *Libre d'Amic e Amat* is not a text intended for continuous reading, but a series of 366 verses or aphorisms, each one of which is sufficient for a whole day's meditation along the lines set out in the *Art de contemplació*. In the preface, Llull explains that the book is composed in the manner of the *sufis*, or Arab mystics, which may account for the fact that the two personages of the dialogue—the lover, or soul in search of mystical union, and the beloved who is his ideal—are each represented by a masculine noun (*Amic, Amat*), in contrast to the bride-bridegroom relationship of other mystical works. As in Llull's fiction, the quest theme lies behind some of the most haunting images:

> Anava l'Amic per una ciutat com a foll cantant de son Amat, e demanaren-li les gents si havia perdut son seny. Respòs que son Amat havia pres son voler, e que ell li havia donat son enteniment; per açò era-li romàs tan solament lo remembrament ab què remembrava son amat.[23]

What is characteristic here is the introduction of certain intellectual terms into the general lyrical pattern. A modern reader may be inclined to see the *Libre d'Amic e Amat* as a series of disconnected prose fragments interspersed with more abstract reflections. But if one relates what is being said to the system of ideas which Llull expounds in his other writings, the effect is very different. There are very few verses, in fact, which do not refer in one way or another to the operation of the three powers of the soul—memory, understanding, and will—which appear in the passage just quoted;[24] if one reads the book in this way, one finds that every verse contributes, separately and in combination, to a single total pattern which conveys the essence of Llull's theological speculations. Because of this, the *Libre d'Amic e Amat* embodies with dazzling accuracy what is perhaps Llull's central insight, that in the search for God, love and understanding are equally necessary:

> Tant amava l'Amic son Amat, que de tot ço que li deia lo creia, e tant lo desijava entendre, que tot ço que n'oïa dir

volia entendre per raons necessàries. E per açò l'amor de l'Amic estava entre creença e intel.ligència.[25]

After the *Libre d'Amic e Amat*, Llull's metrical verse may seem disappointing. In his early years, he had written secular poems in the troubadour manner; later, he saw himself as a spiritual *joglar*:

L'art, Sènyer, de joglaria començà en vós a loar e en vós a beneir; e per açò foren atrobats estruments e voltes e lais e sons novells amb què home s'alegràs en vós.[26]

The language of his poetry is closer to Catalan than that of the troubadours, though it preserves the link with Provençal, as well as the metrical variety of troubadour verse. Even his best poems, however, suffer from monotony of rhyme: it is clear that Llull valued metre and rhyme chiefly as aids to memory, and the greater part of his poetry, in fact, is purely didactic in intention. Yet even his most pedestrian verses contain passages which are memorable in a literary sense, and three or four of his poems rise to a far higher level of achievement. Several are original re-workings of established forms; thus, the *Concili*, addressed to the Council of Vienne (1311-12), is a lively combination of the *sirventes* and the crusading song, and the *Plant de Nostra Dona Santa Maria*, which contains some of his most powerful descriptive writing, belongs to the traditional genre of the *Planctus Mariae*.[27]

Llull's finest poems, the *Desconhort* ('Comfortlessness') and the *Cant de Ramon*, are both autobiographical. The *desconhortz* was a recognised troubadour genre, and Llull's poem is written in alexandrines, to be sung 'al so de Berard', i.e. to the tune of an epic poem of the Carolingian cycle. The poem, which runs to over 800 lines, takes the form of a debate between the author himself and a hermit whom he meets in a wood. The prevailing mood is one of depression and self-doubt: in the course of the dialogue, the hermit reproaches Llull for the failure of his missionary plans and accuses him of overambitiousness and pride. Both speakers are clearly aspects of Llull's own temperament, and the strength of the poem lies in the absolute honesty with which Llull puts his spiritual motives to the test. In the end, the hermit is convinced by the author's self-defence, and the two leave in separate directions, as friends engaged in the same spiritual enterprise.

This symbolic restoration of mental equilibrium is a genuine victory over the doubts which Llull must have experienced at many stages in his career. The *Cant de Ramon* (1299), though briefer and more economical, reflects another similar moment with complete frankness and humility:

> Som hom vell, paubre, menyspreat,
> no hai ajuda d'home nat
> e hai trop gran fait emparat.
> Gran res hai de lo mon cercat;
> mant bon eximpli hai donat:
> poc som conegut e amat.[28]

The next line, however, plunges abruptly into the world of mystical experience: 'Vull morir en pèlag d'amor'.[29] This note recurs throughout the poem, especially in the lines which refer to the founding of the monastery of Miramar, the symbol of all Llull's missionary endeavours:

> Lo monestir de Miramar
> feu a Frares Menors dar,
> per sarraïns a predicar.
> Enfre la vinya e'l fenollar
> amor me pres, fe'm Déus amar
> enfre sospirs e plors estar.[30]

The vine and the fennel, sighs and tears; elsewhere, love and the lack of love, faith and intelligence. Llull's mind seems to work most naturally in terms of such polarities; an argumentative mind which knows, nevertheless, that the greatest truths can only be communicated through the imagination and the spirit.

*   *   *

One contemporary figure is often linked with Llull: that of the

Valencian, Arnau de Vilanova (*c.* 1237-1311), who achieved international fame as both a physician and religious visionary. As Professor of Medicine at Montpellier and personal doctor to a series of kings and popes, he enjoyed enormous prestige, and his appeal to reason and experience in medical treatment, based on a combination of Galen and Arabic teaching, retained its authority until the eighteenth century. His spiritual activities were much more controversial, and complicated, as in the case of Llull, by his direct knowledge of Muslim and Jewish practices. Beyond this, there is very little resemblance between the two men: where Llull is contemptuous of the less orthodox religious movements of the time, Arnau de Vilanova was strongly influenced both by the Franciscan Spirituals and by the wave of messianism which swept the Jewish communities of Europe in 1295. In the last fifteen years of his life, he seems to have devoted himself almost entirely to the propagation of his beliefs concerning the imminent coming of the Apocalypse and the urgency of religious reform. Having met with hostility and indifference in Paris and Rome, he pinned his hopes on the Royal House of Aragon, and on the Court of Frederick III of Sicily, for whom he wrote the *Informació espiritual* (1310), a treatise on the qualities of the ideal Christian ruler, which was used as the basis for the *Constitutions* of Sicily.

Apart from the *Informació* and a pair of letters to royal patrons, only three of Arnau's works in Catalan have survived: the *Confessió de Barcelona* (1305), an exposition of his millennial beliefs, delivered in the presence of Jaume II and the Catalan Court; the *Lliçó de Narbona* (1305-08), a sermon on the evangelical idea of poverty preached to the Beguines of Narbonne; and the *Raonament d'Avinyó* (1310), a defence of the Beguines and the Spirituals which comes close at times to the missionary ideals of Llull. This small handful of texts in itself represents a considerable literary achievement: the lack of spiritual criteria which leads Arnau to accept all kinds of false prophecies and oracles is relatively unimportant, compared with the impact of a compelling personality who manipulates the language with superb oratorical skill. At its most serious, Arnau's style probably owes a great deal to his experience in writing Latin, and here, at least, there is a sense of grammatical strictness, of logical articulation, which looks forward to Eiximenis (see below, pp. 31-2). What is even more striking, however, is the extraordinary vigour and flexibility of a language which can turn from the exalted to the mundane in a single sentence, as when he describes the enforced humility of the Spirituals,

aixì com perles en arena, e moxons en barça d'espines, e tortres en selva, per la multitud e.l poder dels adversaris.[31]

As with Llull, though on a much smaller scale, one is continually surprised by the maturity and variety of a literary language for which there are no surviving precedents.

IV. THE FOUR CHRONICLES

If Llull is an isolated genius and Arnau de Vilanova an interesting eccentric, the more normal kind of literary activity is represented by the four great chronicles which, in the absence of any major fiction or poetry, fill the gap between Llull and the humanistic movement of the late fourteenth century. The strong dynastic sense which made the monastery of Ripoll an early centre of historiography in Latin could hardly have failed to affect vernacular literature.[32] What is particularly striking, however, is that two of the major Catalan chronicles, those of Jaume I and Pere III, are virtually royal autobiographies.

The *Libre dels feyts* of Jaume I (1213-76) is written entirely in the first person. Its textual history is complicated, though the directness and intimacy of many of its best passages leave no doubt as to the intervention of the king himself. As for the process of composition, it seems certain that the original materials were set down by Jaume and his collaborators shortly after the capture of Valencia in 1238. The early part, which consists largely of Jaume's memories of the Valencian campaign and the earlier conquest of Mallorca (1229), was completed in its original form by 1244. Much later, possibly in 1265, the chronicle was resumed and eventually brought up to the year 1274, a time-sequence which accounts for the relatively confused description of events between 1240 and 1265. This original text has not survived: in 1313, at the orders of Jaume II, it was translated into Latin by Petrus Marsilius, who added the final part and divided the whole work into chapters; the definitive Catalan version was then completed, probably in 1327, by imposing the structure of the Latin text on that of the original and by incorporating various stylistic revisions and amplifications introduced by the Latin translator.

The *Libre dels feyts* is a personal chronicle in more senses than one. The 'deeds' of the title are for the most part the military actions accomplished by the king and his armies; little space is given to diplomacy, and there are none of the outbursts of patriotism one finds in Desclot and Muntaner. As against this, there is a strong sense of the workings of Providence and of the value which lies in recording individual feats of heroism. Both themes are handled with a notable lack of exaggeration: if God appears to favour the Catalans, there are no spectacular interventions of the supernatural, and the bravery of the Catalan troops is set firmly in a background of detailed strategies. This relative objectivity is remarkable in a chronicle which conveys so much epic feeling: what controls the description of events, of course, is the temperament of the narrator who is at the same time chief protagonist. There is no doubt that Jaume I was familiar with the values of epic poetry, and passages like those which describe his pride in possessing a sword which had belonged to the Cid, or his courageous behaviour after being wounded in the siege of Valencia, show how closely he modelled his own attitudes on those of the epic heroes. The point is rather that such attitudes are made to seem only part of a much more complex vision of events which ranges from the trivial to the frankly confessional. At either level, the results can be extraordinarily direct:

E fom a Borriana. E quan venc que'n volguem levar la host, una oreneta havia feit niu prop de l'escudella, en lo tendal; e manam que no'n levassen la tenda tro que ella se'n fos anada ab sos fills, pus en nostra fe era venguda.[33]

Or, at a crucial point in the campaign against Valencia:

Ab tant anam nos gitar, e no volguem descobrir les paraules a null hom que fos ab nos. E ja fos en temps de gener, que fa gran fret, contornam nos, la nuyt, més de cent vegades e'l lit, de la primera part de l'altra, e suavem també com si fossem en un bany.[34]

Almost every page of the *Libre dels feyts* is stamped by its author's powers of observation and by the psychological truth of his reactions. In comparison, the chronicle of Desclot, written between 1283 and 1288, is much less vivid, though its language is vigorous and supple, and its account of events highly detailed. The author himself remains a shadowy figure: his identity is still uncertain, though it is clear from the text that he was a well-educated member of the Catalan Court, with easy access to official documents. This anonymity, in fact, seems to have been deliberate: what matters, for Desclot, are the facts themselves, not their interpretation, and this objectivity is translated into a literary formula: 'Ara lexa a parlar lo libre (de tal cosa) e torna a parlar (de tal altra)'.[35]

His chronicle begins in the time of Ramon Berenguer IV (1131-1162), but, apart from the first fifty chapters, is entirely concerned with the reign of Pere II (1276-85). Like the *Libre dels feyts*, the early chapters make use of existing verse material, with a marked preference for the chivalresque and the fantastic, as in the legendary account of the birth of Jaume I, used also by Muntaner.[36] The real protagonist of the chronicle, however, is Pere II, and the principal events it records are the Catalan–Aragonese intervention in southern Italy and the unsuccessful French invasion of Catalonia. It is clear that Desclot's patriotic feelings are directed towards the king himself, rather than towards his dynasty or his country. Perhaps the greatest triumph of the chronicle lies in the skill with which it dramatises the growth of the king's authority from adolescence to maturity. Here, particularly, Desclot shows the impartiality and sense of moral justice which run through his entire work. Though his admiration for Pere II is very great, he makes no attempt to pass over his moral weaknesses or the atrocities which he commits in the war against the French. The same honesty appears in some of his minor portraits, notably in that of the great admiral, Roger de Llúria, whose laconic speeches are among the most memorable things in the book. Like Muntaner, Desclot has a strong antipathy towards the French, though this does not prevent him from praising the noble qualities of their leaders. Compared with the *Libre dels feyts*, Desclot shows more concern for the spirit of chivalry, and it is obvious that Pere II himself at times went out of his way to appear in a chivalresque light, as in the famous episode of the challenge of Bordeaux (1283). What pleases Desclot, however, is the contrast between the oversophistication of the French and the tough simplicity of the Catalans. When Pere returns from Bordeaux, having triumphed over the treachery of Charles d'Anjou, he is seen

> tot sol en son cavall, ab les armes e'l dors; e fou tot suat e colrat del solell e del calor qui era molt gran.[37]

The same contrast appears in the chronicle of Ramon Muntaner (1265-1336), written between 1325 and 1328. At the time of the French invasion of Catalonia in 1285, Muntaner was twenty; he himself describes the sacking of his native town, Peralada:

> Que jo e d'altres que en aquella hora hi perderen, hi perdem gran res d'açò que havíem, e no hi som pus tornats per habitar, ans som anats per lo món cercant consell amb molt mal e molt treball e molts perills que n'havem passats, e dels quals la major part ne són morts en les guerres aquestes que la Casa d'Aragó ha haüdes.[38]

In the course of his wanderings, Muntaner became an important actor in the historical events he was eventually to record. In 1300 he went to Sicily, where he took part in the siege of Messina and became administrator to Roger de Flor, the ex-Templar who two years later commanded the Catalan military expedition to Constantinople. He himself took part in the campaigns in Greece and Asia Minor and for several years was commander of the garrison at Gallipoli. Though in his later years he was involved in a number of important acts of diplomacy, the chief historical interest of his chronicle is the unique account it gives of the expedition to the Near East. As far as objectivity goes, the contrast with Desclot could hardly be greater. Muntaner writes first and foremost as a military leader, whose literary culture is drawn mainly from the Bible, troubadour poetry, and the romances of chivalry. Though his narrative runs from the birth of Jaume I to the coronation of Alfons III (1328), it concentrates chiefly on the French invasion of 1285 and his own experience of the Near Eastern campaign.

Of all the chronicles, this is the most personal; in the prologue, Muntaner relates how an old man appeared to him in a dream, saying 'Muntaner, leva sus, e pensa de fer un libre de les grans meravelles que has vistes'.[39] His engaging lack of modesty comes from the sense of his own value as a unique observer of unparalleled events. It is perhaps symptomatic that he always refers to his work as a 'book' and never as a 'chronicle': certainly, the effect is of a book of memoirs which at the same time is intended to serve as a 'mirror for princes'. This comes out both in his constant appeals to an audience (his favourite narrative formula is 'Què us diré?'—'What can I say to you?') and in his enthusiastic praise of the Aragonese dynasty. Unlike Desclot, he sometimes distorts or omits important episodes, or describes in great detail events at which he was not present. Such lapses from truth are often a condition of his brilliance as a narrator; at a deeper level, however, it is clear that Muntaner was attempting to give an impression of imperial unity at a time when the Catalan–Aragonese domains were in serious danger of disintegrating. And on top of this, there is another problem which must have caused him particular difficulty as a Christian: the fact that several of his masters, like Pere II, had been excommunicated and had fought against the Church. In practice, by skilful manipulation of the facts, Muntaner upholds the infallibility of Rome and at the same time gives an account of events which completely discredits the authority of a particular pope, Martin IV, whose unworthy conduct is shown to be largely responsible for Pere II's bad relations with the Curia. Like the *Libre dels feyts*, though in the face of increasing difficulties, the chronicle of Muntaner succeeds in giving a providential account of history in which the achievements of the House of Aragon are enveloped at times in an atmosphere of Old Testament grandeur.

The last of the four chronicles, that of Pere III (Peter the Ceremonious), is very different from the others. In the first place, its general conception is much more sophisticated: its author is not only an able politician, but also one of the outstanding cultural figures of his time, a superb orator and letter-writer, as well as a minor poet. Above all, Pere III is a king with a passion for history (the *Libre del feyts* was one of his favourite books), and a clear sense of the value of historical writing as a means of justifying imperial policy. Secondly, though his chronicle resembles the *Libre dels feyts* in its autobiographical aspect, it owes much more to contemporary documents, so much so that whole sections of it are little more than diary entries based on the lists of events drawn up by the royal assistants. Its content is divided into seven chapters or books, beginning with the king's birth in 1319 and ending in 1382, five years before his death. Within each chapter, the distribution of material is more selective than in any of the other chronicles, and is generally focused on a single major episode. Thus the third and longest deals with the reincorporation of Mallorca in the kingdom of Aragon and the fourth with the War of the Union against the rebel nobles of Aragon and Valencia. In a letter written to his principal collaborator, Bernat Descoll, in 1375, Pere expresses the wish that 'all facts should be mentioned, though some may be to our discredit'. Clearly, he hoped that even his most violent actions would in the long term be seen as part of a providential design; in practice, the effect of such honesty provides the chronicle with scenes of breathtaking callousness. From a literary point of view, the same directness accounts for the brilliance of many of the individual portraits, notably those of Peter the Cruel and Bertrand du Guesclin, and also for the extraordinary sense of detail which runs through the whole chronicle:

> Apres poc temps venc allí [a Barcelona] l'infant En Jaume, fort mal aparellat de malaltia, en tant com nós li isquem a rebre'l, com entràvem en la ciutat, un hom faia jocs per alegria, que passava e anava de part a part del carrer per un fil prim. E nós li diguem:—Frare, veets aquests jocs?—E ell dix:— Senyor, no veig res—. E tantost com fo en la posada sua, gità's en son lit, e, a cap d'alguns jorns, reté la ànima a nostre senyor Déu.[40]

Each of the four major chronicles is unique in its way, despite certain common features of style. In the long run, however, what marks off the chronicle of Pere III so sharply from the others has nothing to do with literary qualities: it is quite simply the awareness that the nature of government is changing. Just as Catalan culture in the second half of the fourteenth century is beginning to feel the first effects of the Italian Renaissance, so the chronicle of Pere III reflects the way in which medieval political structures are reluctantly yielding to a newer and more absolutist conception of monarchy which comes to rely increasingly on the support of the middle classes in its struggle against the aristocracy.

V. EIXIMENIS, METGE, CANALS

Inevitably, the shift in the sources of power is reflected in the best writers of the late fourteenth century. One cannot help noticing how many prose works of the time are aimed at a middle-class audience. This explains, for instance, why the reign of Pere III is a great age of translation, and why so much four-teenth-century religious writing is concerned with everyday morals and the nature of the urban community. The most instructive example here is Francesc Eiximenis (*c.* 1340-1409), a Franciscan friar who achieved a position of great influence at Court and for many years played a leading part in the administration of Valencia.

Eiximenis's major work is *Lo Crestià*, an encyclopaedic treatise on Christian society. Apart from its vast scale (of the thirteen books originally planned, only four were written, though these in themselves comprise 2,587 chapters), what strikes one in *Lo Crestià* is its absolute faithfulness to the scholastic tradition. In his basic arguments, and in his occasional credulity, Eiximenis is medieval in the most conventional sense: he has none of the sophistication of Llull, and his guarded attitude to the classics sets him apart from a slightly later writer like Bernat Metge. For a modern reader (and, one imagines, for many of his contemporaries) the great attraction of his work lies in the vivid presentation of fourteenth-century society which fills out the scholastic framework. This rich social vision is a direct consequence of the author's intention to write not only for the highly educated, but also for 'the simple layman with no great learning' ('persones simples e legues e sens grans lletres'). His attempt to engage the interest of non-specialist readers accounts for the presence of so many details of public and private life, and also for the vigorous simplicity of the language, as in his description of corrupt princes:

> E fan de la llei tela d'aranya, que no pot retenir res que sia fort, més reté mosquits e coses sense força.[41]

Though basically his language is sophisticated rather than popular, Eiximenis's mastery of dialogue is equalled only by his contemporary Sant Vicenç Ferrer (see below, p. 32). What gives weight to such incidentals, however, is the way in which they are made to illustrate the general principles of a Christian state.

Despite his constant references to Aristotle and St Augustine, there is no doubt that Eiximenis's political and social theories are based on observation: the city which he describes is a real one—Valencia or Barcelona—and he sees the Crown of Aragon as part of a Christendom whose unity, at the time of writing, is flawed by the Papal Schism.

Recent historians have praised the insight with which he sees *pactisme* (rule by mutual agreement) as the distinguishing feature of the Catalan political tradition.[42] He is aware, moreover, that such a tradition can only be maintained with a good deal of effort and mutual trust, and that the royal council of his day is going through a crisis because of the conflicting interests of the city councillors and the king's officials. More often than not, Eiximenis appears to share the urban middle-class mentality of the readers whom he is addressing, as in his undisguised contempt for the peasants. Nevertheless, his position as a friar, and his personal experience as an administrator, enable him to range with confidence over the whole social spectrum. If all political power comes ultimately from God, he argues, the prince is the head of the Christian republic, whose strength lies partly in the integrity of his noble advisers, and partly in his willingness to respect the opinion of his lesser subjects through the machinery of pacts. One of the constant themes in his work is the need to encourage the usefulness of every member of the state, even the physically disabled. And at every point, whether he is speaking of the dignity of labour or of the education of the ideal prince, he is able to appeal to scholastic authority with a simplicity of religious belief which never seems to conflict with his strong sense of practical values.

Such confidence is becoming rarer by the end of the fourteenth century, though one finds it still in the sermons of the Dominican Sant Vicenç Ferrer (1350-1419), an extraordinary example of a sophisticated theologian who deliberately creates a popular idiom in order to communicate with an uneducated public.[43] By 1400, however, a new spirit is beginning to make itself felt in another sector of Catalan prose. Here again, the decisive period is the reign of Pere III. In the first half of the fourteenth century, the vernacular works of Llull continue to act as a criterion for later prose-writers; in the second half of the century, precisely at a time when Llull's reputation is beginning to wane, linguistic uniformity is maintained by the increasing importance of the Royal Chancellory. The reform of the chancellory under Pere III had literary consequences which could hardly have been foreseen at the time. The formation of a group of royal notaries, skilled in writing Latin, Catalan, and Aragonese, coincided with the growing demand for translations from classical Latin. At first, such classics were valued chiefly for their moral content; eventually, however, in the early 1380s, there comes a stage at which certain stylistic tendencies begin to emerge, notably the attempt to adapt Ciceronian prose to the vernacular. This aesthetic revaluation of prose on the part of a group of professional writers with a taste for classical culture led to a new type of humanism which is sometimes referred to as the Catalan Pre-Renaissance. The presiding figure in this movement is not Pere III but his successor, Joan I (1387-95), whose marriage to Violant de Bar and relations with the Court of Avignon brought Catalonia for a time into the cultural orbit of France. And, significantly, it is Joan I who is the protagonist of the one masterpiece which the movement produced, the *Somni* of Bernat Metge.

Bernat Metge (*ante* 1346-1413) was closely involved in the events of the time. His stepfather, Fernan Sayol, was chief notary to Eleanor of Sicily, the third wife of Pere III; his translation of the *De re rustica* of Palladius Rutilius and his early interest in Cicero established him as a respectable minor humanist, and it seems likely that his literary tastes had a strong influence on Metge himself. The latter joined the chancellory and continued to serve under his friend and literary patron Joan I. After the sudden death of the king in 1395, Metge was accused, along with a number of other officials, of administrative corruption, and probably imprisoned. Shortly afterwards, he was rehabilitated, and eventually became secretary to the new king, Martí I.

Most of Bernat Metge's literary work was composed between

1381 and 1399, and it shows very clearly the transition from medievalism to something distinctly more modern. His allegorical poem, the *Llibre de Fortuna e Prudència* (1381), poses the question of Providence in purely medieval terms, with obvious debts to Boethius and the *Roman de la rose*. The *Història de Valter e Griselda*, written seven years later, is very different: a translation of Petrarch's Latin version of a story from the *Decameron*. This may seem a perverse way of translating Boccaccio; its real significance, however, lies in the excellent and novelty of its prose and in the fact that its preface contains the first eulogy of Petrarch by a Peninsular writer. Metge's praise, significantly, is for Petrarch the Latin humanist, not for the vernacular poet, and it is this aspect of the older author which comes to dominate his own literary work. In 1395, shortly before the death of Joan I, he spent some time at the Papal Court in Avignon, where he met the famous Aragonese humanist Juan Fernández de Heredia, and almost certainly read the *Secretum* of Petrarch, a powerful confessional dialogue composed at a time of intense spiritual crisis. Metge's own *Apologia*, written under the first impact of the *Secretum*, is an early, over-literary attempt to adapt the Ciceronian dialogue to his own language; in retrospect, however, it reads like a first sketch for his masterpiece, *Lo somni* (1399).

The *Somni* is divided into four books. In the first, the ghost of Joan I appears to Bernat Metge in prison, accompanied by Orpheus and Tiresias. The king's own situation (it emerges that he is in Purgatory for having condoned the Papal Schism) leads to a discussion concerning the immortality of the soul, and in the second book the dialogue hinges on the circumstances of the author's own political disgrace. In the third, Orpheus and Tiresias, who symbolise the king's love of music and astrology, tell their own stories, and the latter delivers an angry diatribe against women; in the final book, Metge replies with a defence of the famous women of antiquity, ending with a passage in praise of the new queen, Maria de Luna, and a satire against the vices of men.

The greater part of the *Somni* is based directly on passages from other authors, among them Cicero, Valerius Maximus, Boccaccio, and the Church Fathers. What saves it from being a mere plagiarism is the author's own intellectual attitude. The humanistic note is struck early in the first book: 'hom són així com los altres, e cové que seguesca llurs petjades'.[44] In practice, this amounts to a combination of generosity and scepticism: generosity in the sense of friendship which colours the relationship between the author and his dead master, scepticism in his reluctance to go beyond the evidence of his senses. The liveliness of the opening dialogue depends to a great extent on the constant questioning of the king's present state and, though in the end Metge allows himself to be won over by the Christian arguments for immortality, it is his scepticism which really convinces:

> Bé saps tu [says the king] que moltes coses creu hom, que no pot veure.—Ver és—diguí jo—mas no els tenc per savis aquells qui n'usen. Ço que veig crec, e del pus no cur.[45]

If this sceptical *persona* raises the *Somni* above the level of a literary exercise, much of its urgency comes from the immediate circumstances of its composition. It is clear that, in writing it, Metge was not so much concerned with the immortality of the soul or the denunciation of vices, as with justifying his own actions. One of his motives for writing in Catalan, one suspects, was the desire to make his self-defence available to any educated reader, and to one reader in particular, Martí I. One can only admire the strategy by which he enlists the support of the dead king, and, judged by its practical results, his defence appears to have been completely successful. From a literary point of view, an immense distance separates Bernat Metge from a writer like Eiximenis. The polish and restraint of *Lo somni* are quite new to Catalan prose and, if its tone reminds one at times of Montaigne, this is merely the way of observing the real, though limited, extent to which it anticipates the Renaissance.

Though Bernat Metge is the most talented of the Catalan humanists, his scepticism reflects a more general tendency to rationalism of which other writers of the time were aware. One

finds a very different reaction, for example, in the work of
Antoni Canals (c. 1352-1419), the eminent Dominican and
translator of Valerius Maximus, Seneca, and Petrarch. Intellec-
tually, Canals is closer to Eiximenis than to Bernat Metge, but
unlike Eiximenis, he deliberately sets out to fight the sceptics
with their own weapons. His strictly religious works, the *Escala
de contemplació* and the *Tractat de confessió*, show a nostalgia
for the contemplative life, conceived in terms of the Dominican
mystical tradition. In the prefaces to the classical translations,
however, he clearly hopes that those readers who no longer
acknowledge the authority of the Bible will be attracted to the
Christian virtues by the example of the classical moralists. Thus,
he dedicates his version of the *De providentia* of Seneca to the
Governor of Valencia, Ramon Boyl, with the words:

> no em direu que lo dit Sèneca sia profeta ni patriarca, qui
> parlen figurativament, ans lo trobarets tot filòsof, qui funda
> son fet en juy e raó natural.[46]

Canals, in fact, never allows his sense of classical values to conflict with his religious faith. If he is a less original author than
Bernat Metge, this is partly because he never sees himself as a
literary writer. His aim is quite simply 'to create the perfect and
finished man' ('fer l'hom perfecte e acabat'): not Renaissance
Man, but a Christian humanist who will embody the best values
of medieval orthodoxy and classical antiquity. In this, of course,
he is close to Petrarch himself, and it is the example of Petrarch's
Latin writings which, more than anything, gives an appearance
of unity to the series of minor humanists and translators who
follow one another almost until the end of the fifteenth century.

VI. POETRY FROM LLULL TO ROIÇ DE CORELLA

Compared with the achievement of fourteenth-century prose,
the poetry of the same period is on the whole dull and repetitive.
The main reason for this lies in the tyranny of the Provençal

tradition. Llull, as we saw, continues to use the language of troubadour poetry, though his aims are quite different. After him, the same tradition was maintained, with none of Llull's originality, as a consciously artificial kind of writing, increasingly divorced from the vital centres of Catalan culture. This process is paralleled in the south of France. Just as the first organisation of troubadour poets, the *Sobregaia companhia dels set trobadors*, was set up at Toulouse in 1323, with a complicated apparatus of rules and prizes, so, seventy years later, the *Consistori de la gaia ciència* was founded in Barcelona, with very similar intentions. The effect of this was to confirm the general stagnation of serious poetry in Catalonia which had come about earlier in the fourteenth century. There is nothing to compare here with the way in which Italian poetry was able to develop through the *stil nuovo* to Dante and Petrarch, nor with the innovations of French poets like Machaut and Alain Chartier. Even so, there are some interesting exceptions. The only fourteenth-century collection of poems to have survived, the *Cançoneret de Ripoll*, contains a number of more popular pieces, notably those by the Capellà de Bolquera (late thirteenth century?) and the anonymous lament which begins:

> Lassa! Mais m'hagra valgut
> que fos maridada,
> o cortès amic hagut,
> que can sui monjada.[47]

These poems, significantly, are written in Catalan, not Provençal, and the same is true of a number of satirical poems which have survived from the later part of the century, like the anonymous *Disputació d'En Buc e son cavall*, the *Sermó* of Bernat Metge, and the *Elogi dels diners* of Anselm Turmeda.

This, then, is the situation in Catalan poetry around 1400: Provençal is still being maintained, with increasing difficulty, as an artificial language, but against this one has to set the rather timid beginnings of a satirical poetry in Catalan. And, curiously enough, the courtly love tradition, after remaining sterile for over a century, is going through a successful minor revival, partly through Italian influence, in the work of poets like Gilabert de Pròixita, Melcior Gualbes, and Andreu Febrer (*c.* 1375-*c.* 1444), one of the earliest translators of the *Divine Comedy.*

The finest representative of this moment is Jordi de Sant Jordi, a Valencian aristocrat who died in 1425, still in his twenties. Unlike the more conventional poets of his time, Jordi de Sant Jordi wrote love-poems which are both moving and elegantly phrased—so much so, that it is tempting to say that all the tradition needed, even at this late stage, was a poet of sufficient talent and personality. How Jordi de Sant Jordi might have developed had he lived longer, one can only guess. The poems he managed to write show him still using a slightly Catalanised form of Provençal, still moving very consciously within the orbit of troubadour poetry, though with occasional touches which suggest that he had read Petrarch. More important, the courtly attitudes of his poems seem to reflect his own circumstances. Like Andreu Febrer and his Castilian contemporary, the future marqués de Santillana (1398-1458), Jordi de Sant Jordi was a member of the Court of Alfons IV (Alfonso the Magnanimous), and, along with Febrer and Ausias March, took part in the expedition to Corsica and Sardinia of 1420. In 1423, he was captured and imprisoned for a short time in Naples, an event which is recorded in one of his most successful poems, the *Presoner.* Even in those poems which are not related to particular occasions, one is struck by the same sense of individual experience which breaks free from the topics of courtly poetry. His love-poems are surprisingly free from abstractions: in the best of them, the *Stramps* (or unrhymed verses), the opening lines pick up a conceit used by earlier troubadour poets, and turn it into a statement of great force and dignity:

> Jus lo front port vostra bella semblança,
> de què mon cors nit e jorn fa gran festa,
> que remiran la molt bella figura

de vostra faç m'és romansa l'empremta
que ja per mort no se'n partrà la forma,
ans quan seray tot fors d'est segle,
ells qui lo cors portaran al sepulcre
sobre ma faç veuran lo vostre signe.[48]

Such a poem is a fine achievement in itself, and confirms the
later judgement of the marqués de Santillana: 'Compuso asaz
fermosas cosas, las cuales él mismo asonava, ca fué músico
excelente'. One can only regret the loss of the musical settings,
though the texts alone bear witness to a talent which, even if it
does not seriously question the earlier tradition, seems to point
the way to more original possibilities.

The first major poet to write entirely in Catalan is Ausias
March (1397-1459), and it is no coincidence that he is the
greatest poet in the language. The relation of Ausias March to
the courtly tradition is complex and fundamental: roughly
speaking, what he offers is not so much an alternative tradition
as a way out of the existing one, above all in the direction of
introspection and self-awareness. And seen in this light, the
reason for his choice of Catalan seems obvious: the independence of mind which shows through all his best writing positively
demands a language which will remove his poetry at one stroke
from the conventional associations of Provençal.

It is curious that both the father and uncle of Ausias March
were talented, if unadventurous, minor poets, and that his father,
Pere March, was one of the people entrusted with drawing up
the statutes of the *Consistori de la gaia ciència* in 1393. His
family belonged to the minor Valencian nobility, though in fact
it had only been raised to noble status in 1360, and there are
moments in his poems when one detects a lack of confidence in
his social status which contrasts very noticeably with a here-
ditary aristocrat like Jordi de Sant Jordi. Like Jordi de Sant
Jordi, however, Ausias March took part in the wars in Naples,
Sicily, and North Africa in the early 1420s, but in 1425 he
seems to have abandoned his military career, and not long after-

wards he probably wrote his first poems. In his later years, one finds him engaged in the typical activities of a fifteenth-century squire: fighting lawsuits with rich neighbours, administering justice, and raising falcons for the king. In 1437, when he was about forty, he married the sister of Joanot Martorell, the author of *Tirant lo blanc* (see below, p. 50). Two years later, she died, and in 1443 he married a second time. This new marriage lasted eleven years, in the course of which Ausias March took up residence in the city of Valencia. Then, in 1454, his second wife died, five years before the poet himself, and it is possible that her death is directly related to some of his most moving verses.

The blurred impression which comes from the biographical facts contrasts strangely with the very strong sense of personality one finds in the poetry. The poet who can write at the climax of one of his most powerful poems 'Jo só aquest que.m dich Ausias March'[49] needs no biographer to bring out his individuality, and even at their most abstract, his poems give the impression of a living person who is anxiously debating matters which deeply concern him.

Out of a total of 128 poems, about three-quarters are love-poems, most of which are related, directly or indirectly, to the courtly tradition. But taking his work as a whole, there is a good case for calling it 'moral poetry', rather than simply 'love-poetry'. A few poems, in fact, are quite clearly moral poems, which meditate philosophically, and a little predictably, on questions like the nature of virtue and goodness. Much more important than these are the half-dozen poems which centre on death: these poems, which represent Ausias March's supreme achievement, are concerned not merely with death in a general way, but with the death of a particular person, a woman whom the poet has loved in the fullest sense, and inevitably they lead him to thoughts about his own death.

Ausias March's love-poems form a number of cycles, each of which is addressed to a single woman, who is identified in the *envoi* by a pseudonym or *senhal*: 'llir entre cards' ('lily among thorns') or 'plena de seny' ('full of intelligence'), to name the

two most important. Each cycle has its own distinctive features:
thus, the 'plena de seny' poems insist on the woman's ungrate-
fulness, sometimes in derogatory terms; also, though both cycles
introduce the subject of death, this is a much more central
theme in the 'llir entre cards' sequence, which also refers to the
poet's timidity, to his shame at his previous love affairs, and to
the divine nature of the woman concerned.

One of the 'llir entre cards' poems (XXIII) begins:

> Lleixant apart l'estil dels trobadors,
> qui, per escalf, traspassen veritat ...[50]

It would be wrong to take this as a general denunciation of
troubadour poetry: in the context of the whole poem, which is
concerned with praising a particular woman, it is as if the poet
were saying 'We all know that the troubadours are inclined to
exaggerate; what I am about to say is the plain truth'. Yet one
should not underestimate this opening gesture: there can be no
question that, taking the poems as a whole, the kind of introspection they contain goes much deeper than anything one finds
in the troubadours, and that this depth depends to a great extent
on not idealising their subject. In this particular poem, we are
reminded at various moments that, although the woman is a
model of perfection, she is still a human being, and never more
so that when she is told: 'verge no sou perquè Déu ne volc
casta'.[51]

Death, for Ausias March, is bound up with the destructive
power of love and the extreme difficulty of avoiding this. When
he theorises about love, he adopts the threefold division of
spiritual love, animal passion, and *amor mixtus* which runs
through the whole courtly love tradition. Where he goes further
than other poets is in exploring the frontier between the body
and the spirit. If love is a torture, as it so clearly is in many
of his poems, this is not simply a matter of the opposing
natures of body and spirit, but of the way in which these two
natures continually act on one another, so that the flesh tries to

rise into the orbit of the spirit, whereas the spirit is always inclined to demean itself and sink to the level of the flesh. On this view, the kind of compromise implied in *amor mixtus* is bound to fail: the body will always win. In fact, he goes further than this: not only can the body and the spirit never be reconciled, but, he argues, there is a conflict within the spirit itself. Just as the body and the spirit tend to usurp one another's domains, so the spirit is torn apart when love degenerates into the selfish passion of the instincts.

This is the central source of tension in Ausias March, and however he tries to argue himself out of it—and he does this at times with great subtlety—it is something to which he is always forced to return. Because of his tendency to indulge in extended philosophical argument, some critics are inclined to speak of him as a philosophical poet, a writer with a basically intellectual cast of mind. This seems an exaggeration: his accurate knowledge of scholastic theory is surprising in a fifteenth-century Valencian aristocrat, though it hardly goes beyond what one would expect to find in any reasonably educated scholar of the time, and of course it tells us nothing about the quality of the poetry. The main thing is that it gives him a consistent frame of reference within which to analyse his feelings. In his less successful poems, there are disconcerting shifts from concrete, personal passages to abstract, moralising ones, but in his finest work, the combination succeeds magnificently, just because, through the use of allegory in simile, he is able to present his abstractions in concrete terms.

On the one hand, then, his poetry is continually testing personal experience by submitting it to rational analysis. On the other, it is a kind of poetry which often tries to extend that experience by comparing it with other human situations. Here, Ausias March's mind tends to work by analogy: time after time he begins a poem by saying 'I am like the man who ...', or, 'Like one who ... so it is with me'. And it is in this type of poem that we are made most aware of the kind of images which seem to have haunted his mind. These, almost without excep-

tion, are sombre and disturbing: comparisons drawn from the
sickbed, the prison cell, and the dangers of the elements, particularly of his great symbol of turbulence, the sea:

> Bullirà el mar com la cassola en forn,
> mudant color e l'estat natural,
> e mostrarà voler tota res mal
> que sobre si atur un punt al jorn;
> grans e pocs peixs a recors correran
> e cercaran amagatalls secrets:
> fugint al mar, on són nodrits e fets,
> per gran remei en terra eixiran.[52] (XLVI)

The six poems usually known as the *Cants de mort* (XCII-XCVII)
refer to the death of a woman who is quite distinct from those
addressed in the other cycles. The most dramatic of all is the
fifth: here, the poet's grief comes from the fact that he does not
know whether, as he puts it, 'God has taken her to himself',
or whether He has 'buried her in Hell', and because of this
uncertainty, he does not know how to address her. If she is in
Hell, he reflects that he himself may have been the cause of
her damnation:

> Si és així, anul.la'm l'esperit,
> sia tornat mon ésser en no res,
> e majorment si'n lloc tal per mi és;
> no sia jo de tant adolorit.[53]

This is perhaps the most terrible problem of conscience in his
whole work: the idea that he may have brought about another
person's damnation. To whom could these poems possibly be
addressed? In the third of them, he turns to the reader, saying
that those who know that he has previously described sinful
passion will perhaps fail to recognise that he is now writing
about an honest love. In the cycle as a whole, there is no sense
that this was an unattainable love, and in the final poem there
is a moving reference to the woman's dying moments:

Enquer està que vida no finí,
com prop la mort jo la viu acostar,
dient plorant: -No vullau mi leixar,
hajau dolor de la dolor de mi.[54]

If one tries to imagine these poems as referring to any of the
women of the other cycles, the differences stand out immediately; quite simply, it is difficult to conceive this situation as
one which involves another man's wife. Addressing the reader
at another point, Ausias March writes:

Als que la Mort toll la muller aimia
sabran jutjar part de la dolor mia.[55]

The crucial phrase is 'muller aimia': 'loved woman'?, 'beloved
wife'? One cannot be sure, though it is tempting to relate the
poems to the death of the poet's second wife, Joana Scorna, in
1454. If this were true, it would mean that here, in some of the
most moving poetry he ever wrote, Ausias March has left behind
the courtly tradition in a quite unprecedented way.

The *Cants de mort* are poems which attempt to deal with
the possibilities of salvation and damnation, that is to say, with
matters which lie at the centre of Christian belief. In these
particular poems, Ausias March does not try to generalise beyond
the context of the individual relationship. It would be surprising, however, if a poet who questions so much in his own
experience were not equally introspective about his relations
with Christianity, and there is one poem, the *Cant espiritual*
(cv), which sums up a great deal of what we find scattered
through the rest of his work. The whole poem, which runs to
over 200 lines, is cast in the form of a prayer, and the general
sense is quite clear: the speaker wishes to achieve salvation,
but feels that he is too weak to do so without the help of God.
Of all the poems, this is the one which goes furthest along the
line of self-reproach. This is not just a question of confessing
to various sins; it is also a recognition of the poet's failure in

his relations with God. At one point he says 'Jo tem a Tu més que no't só amable',[56] and this inability to feel genuine love for God is at the heart of the poem and its tensions. For one thing, he is caught between his fear of death and the wish to die before he commits any further sins, and for another, he recognises that there can be no possible salvation without love. One critic, Joan Fuster, has claimed that God, for Ausias March, is no more than the basic piece in a moral system, at most a judge, but in no sense the active, personal God of Christianity.[57] One sees what he means, though he is surely oversimplifying. What is clear, here and elsewhere, is Ausias March's total inability to delude himself. Because of the energy of his verse and the intensity of his self-enquiry, the results are never merely negative. One phrase in particular stays in the mind as a superb expression of the state from which so much of his poetry derives: 'en tot lleig fet hagué lo cor salvatge',[58] an appropriate note on which to leave a poet whose sheer intelligence and energy enabled him to use the existing tradition to produce great poetry.

*   *   *

Like Ausias March, the two other important poets of the fifteenth century, Jaume Roig and Roiç de Corella, are both Valencians. This points to a striking feature of the literary scene after about 1450: the tendency, in poetry at least, to divide into separate schools. Thus, the Barcelona poets tend to maintain the courtly love tradition, and at the same time to produce a fairly conventional kind of religious verse, whereas the Valencians concentrate more on satire and what, for want of a better term, one may call the 'humanistic lyric'. Of the two major schools, the Valencian is the more original, and the vitality of its satirical writing continues well into the next century. Its most remarkable exponent is Jaume Roig (c. 1400-78), an eminent physician and city councillor, whose long poem Lo spill ('The mirror') or Llibre de les dones, was written between 1456 and 1461. What immediately strikes one about the Spill is its unusual metre: over 16,000 lines of four or five syllables each, rhyming in couplets:

> Una en penjaren,
> viva escorxaren,
> gran fetillera
> e metzinera.
> De nit venia
> sens companyia,
> sola pujava
> e arrancava
> dents e queixals
> dels qui, en pals
> ben alts muntats,
> eren penjats.[59]

Though the poem is narrated in the first person, it is not autobiographical. The plot is complex and episodic: the protagonist is compelled to live by his wits, and his chief aim in life is to settle down as a respectable married citizen of Valencia. This intention is frustrated by a series of disastrous marriages; the whole book, in fact, consists of a virulent and exhaustive denunciation of women, interspersed with an enormous variety of anecdotes. The many touches of humour are really only incidental: in the long run, few medieval works are so unremittingly pessimistic, and one can only wonder at the apparent gulf which separates the fiction from the known facts of the author's life. The *Spill*, nevertheless, is a remarkable work, and precisely for its fictional qualities: a strange combination of anger and ingenuity which, cast in a different form, might have been the ancestor of the picaresque novel.

The work of Joan Roiç de Corella (*c.* 1438-97) could hardly be more different, in itself a sign of the extraordinary variety of Valencian culture in the second half of the fifteenth century. Roiç de Corella is the last of the great Catalan humanists, and the only outstanding poet of the movement. The greater part of his writings is in prose, and his re-workings of Ovidian fables show a characteristically Renaissance pleasure in the aesthetic possibilities of myth. In his prose, the delight in craftsmanship often produces an intricate and convoluted style quite unlike the relative austerity of earlier Catalan writers. The same is true of his love-poetry: apart from Ausias March, he is the only fifteenth-century poet of importance who succeeds in escaping from the tyranny of the courtly tradition. His early *Tragèdia de Caldesa*, written in a mixture of prose and verse, already reveals a mastery of rhetoric and sensuous detail, and the deception it describes suggests a real situation which appears to lie beneath a number of the later poems. Occasionally, as in the *Balada de la garsa i l'esmerla*, he achieves a simplicity and a delicacy which can compare with the best poetry of the Spanish *cancioneros*. This, however, is rare: more often than not, his love-poetry moves in an atmosphere of solemn ritual and syntactical elaboration, with occasional echoes of Petrarch and other Renaissance poets. As a Master of Theology, Roiç de Corella wrote a number of fairly undistinguished religious works in prose, as well as translating the Psalms and the *Vita Christi* of Ludolphus of Saxony. His religious poems, on the other hand, are impressive whenever their lapidary style is able to combine with the richly sensuous imagery he had learned to use in his translations of Ovid. Thus, in his fine poem on the Descent from the Cross, the *Oració a la Santíssima Verge Maria tenint son fill, Déu Jesús, en la falda*, he describes the mourning universe in almost surrealistic terms:

> crida lo sol plorant ab cabells negres,
> e tots los cels vestits de negra sarga
> porten acords al plant de vostra lengua.[60]

With Roiç de Corella, more than with any other fifteenth-century writer, one begins to see what Catalan Renaissance poetry might have been: the verse line is becoming more flexible, as if in response to Italian metrics, and there is a delight in sensuous effects which can be turned to both secular and religious purposes. But, for reasons which will emerge, such a poetry was never fully realised, and the flowering of Valencian culture, so real while it lasted, was ultimately to prove deceptive.

VII. FIFTEENTH-CENTURY FICTION:

Curial e Güelfa AND *Tirant lo blanc*

Two major works of fiction date from the fifteenth century: the anonymous *Curial e Güelfa* and the *Tirant lo blanc* of Joanot Martorell and Martí de Galba. Both are usually referred to as novels of chivalry, though compared with Castilian examples of the genre such as *Amadís de Gaula* they contain very little fantasy, and the actions of their protagonists, however remarkable, tend to remain within the bounds of credibility. Reading the documents of the time, one is struck by the extent to which chivalresque behaviour dominates the lives of the fifteenth-century aristocracy: the personal feuds and private wars of the Catalan and Valencian nobility are conducted with precisely the kind of ritual described in the novels, in a way which seems to imply a steady interaction of life and literature.[61]

Both novels are concerned with the education of a single knight, a process which is conceived for the most part in practical terms. *Curial e Güelfa*, the less ambitious of the two, survives in a single anonymous manuscript, written sometime between 1435 and 1462 by an author who is familiar with Italian topography, possibly a member of the Neapolitan Court. (In its general lines, and some of its details, it bears a certain resemblance to Antoine de Sale's *Le petit Jehan de Saintré* (1456), notably in the humble background of its hero and in the way he is adopted by a young widow of noble birth.) The preface makes it clear that Curial is to become an exceptional lover, as well as an excellent knight, and the strategy employed by Güelfa, his young patroness, allows for both possibilities:

Ma intenció és fer-lo home, emperò no li entenc donar la
mia amor, sinó treballar en fer-lo prous e valerós donant-li
entendre que l'am.[62]

In personal terms, the purpose of Curial's education is to make
him worthy of Güelfa, whom he eventually marries. Like Tirant,
Curial is emotionally timid and easily tempted by the symbolic-
ally named Laquesis, the daughter of the Duke of Bavaria. The
erotic atmosphere which surrounds Laquesis is one of the
triumphs of the book, as is (for similar reasons) the episode in
which Curial is entertained for the night in a French convent.
Though the manners which the novel records are strictly contemporary, it is also in a sense a historical narrative, since the
action is set in the second half of the thirteenth century, and
the most vivid character of all is Pere II (1276-89), whose
portrait is clearly based on the chronicle of Desclot (see above,
p. 26).

The basic values of the novel are medieval, though there are
times when it approaches the world of fifteenth-century humanism, as in the episode of the visit to Mount Parnassus, a curious
digression which seems at odds with the rest of the book. This
is not the only false note in the novel: Curial's adventures in
North Africa, though vividly described, are neither chivalresque
nor humanistic, and they seem to foreshadow the sentimental
novel without realising its full implications. Taken as a whole,
however, *Curial e Güelfa* is remarkable both for the skill of the
writing and for the way in which it suggests a code of manners
which is beginning to disintegrate. This is partly a question of
verisimilitude: Curial's family is poor and undistinguished, and
he depends on Güelfa, a rich young widow, for economic support; yet, as the King of France recognises, these things do not
exclude a man from the order of chivalry. This more liberal
view, which is opposed by some of the more snobbish characters,
is hardly the traditional one, and it is combined with more
practical considerations: like Tirant, Curial kills no monsters,
and for most of the novel is simply a brilliant military com-

mander. But the most telling criticism of chivalry takes a different form. Sangler, a French knight whom Curial has defeated, reappears later as a monk on Mount Sinai, where he urges Curial to change his own way of life:

> E tu, qui has batallat per les vanitats mundanes, batalla ara contra el diable en defensió de la tua ànima ... Oh catiu! ¿e no et penits de les batalles que has fetes per la vanaglòria del món? Has morts hòmens, has trameses ànimes als inferns.[63]

The voice is almost that of Llull and, though Curial ignores the advice, it points unmistakably to a basic flaw in the chivalresque ideal.

Tirant lo blanc is even less of a novel of chivalry in the conventional sense. Its author, Joanot Martorell (*c.* 1410-68), seems to have been a typical member of the Valencian nobility, quarrelsome, aggressive, and continually involved in personal feuds which took him at different stages in his career to both England and Portugal. His only other known work, *Guillem de Varoic*, is partly incorporated in the early chapters of *Tirant lo blanc*; the *Tirant* itself was begun around 1460 and completed after the author's death by Martí Joan de Galba, whose contribution was probably fairly slight. Cervantes's opinion of the novel is well-known:

> por su estilo es éste el mejor libro del mundo; aquí comen los caballeros y duermen, y mueren en sus camas, y hacen testamento antes de su muerte, con otras cosas de que todos los demás libros de este género carecen. (*Don Quixote* I, vi)

The realism which struck Cervantes is one of the most consistent features of the novel. Roughly speaking, the *Tirant* is the story of an imaginary knight, whose greatest achievement is to deliver Constantinople from the threat of the Turks. After the early scenes, which take place at the English Court, the action centres on the Mediterranean. Tirant, by now a famous general, takes part in the French expedition to Rhodes and becomes commander-in-chief of the Byzantine armies; later, after a series of adventures in North Africa, he returns to Constantinople, marries the Emperor's daughter, Carmesina, and dies of an illness shortly afterwards. Though the novel contains many references to historical fact (the character of Tirant, for example, seems partly modelled on Roger de Flor), it never mentions the actual Fall of Constantinople of 1453, as if the plausibility of the action were intended to suggest the possibility of an imminent reconquest.

Like *War and Peace*, the *Tirant* includes enough material for several lesser novels. Apart from its immense value as a document on the fifteenth-century art of war, it offers a sympathetic, though clear-sighted, commentary on the whole ethos of chivalry, as well as comprising a love story of great subtlety and originality. It is clear that the manners and customs of the Byzantine Court are an accurate reflection of those of Valencia, though Martorell's realism is so convincing that it is often difficult to say where his social observation gives way to invention. One of the most striking features of this society is its love of ritual, which affects everything from personal relationships to the elaborate protocol which surrounds the most brutal behaviour. The common factor in all this is language: the characters of the *Tirant* take as much pleasure in drawing up an elegantly worded challenge as in postponing their sexual pleasures with fine talk. And in both areas of experience, ritual is linked with strategy: not only detailed schemes for defeating one's enemy in war, but also the deliberate manipulation of potential sexual partners.

As Frank Pierce has observed, sex in the *Tirant* has more to do with courtly life than with courtly love.[64] Many episodes in the book would be merely pornographic, were it not for the humour and naturalness with which they are presented. What is surprising is the frequent juxtaposition of the erotic and the spiritual, as when Tirant conceives eternal love for Carmesina after an accidental glimpse of her breasts:

E per la gran calor que feia, ... les finestres tancades, estava

mig descordada mostrant en los pits dues pomes de paradís
... les quals donaren entrada als ulls de Tirant, que d'allí
avant no trobaren per on eixir, e totstemps foren apresonats
en poder de persona lliberta, fins que la mort dels dos féu
separació.[65]

At a moment like this, Martorell still preserves a measure of
courtly elegance; sometimes, however, this kind of situation
becomes sheer farce, as in the scene where Plaerdemavida, the
lady-in-waiting, smuggles Tirant into Carmesina's bed and pro-
ceeds to warn him whenever her mistress shows signs of waking.
Plaerdemavida, in fact, is memorable largely because she com-
bines the greatest freedom in sexual matters with the highest
degree of personal chastity. The most corrupt person in the book
is the ageing Empress of Constantinople, who at one point conceals the young squire Hipòlit in her bedroom for fifteen days;
later, after the Emperor's death, she marries him, though significantly referring to him as 'mon fill'. In this and other episodes,
the *Tirant* comes close to suggesting the existence of the sub-
conscious, particularly in the importance it attaches to dreams,
both real and pretended. One especially striking example of
this also brings out the author's subtlety as a narrator. In
chapters 162-3, we are told how Carmesina and Estefania arrange
to spend the night in the palace with their lovers, Tirant and
Diafebus, while Plaerdemavida spies on them through a key-
hole. At first, the actions of the lovers are not described: all we
know is that they spend the night together and separate at dawn.
Only later does Plaerdemavida reveal to the two other women
that she has been an eyewitness, and this she does indirectly,
by claiming that she has seen everything in a dream. Throughout the whole episode, Martorell keeps the reader in suspense
with masterly skill, not the least by his inversion of the natural
order of events.

This pleasure in narrative technique is one of the great
strengths of the novel, and is more sophisticated than anything
in earlier Peninsular fiction.[66] Martorell moves easily between

humanistic prose and familiar dialogue, and any literary influences are completely assimilated. What makes parts of the *Tirant* seem so strikingly modern, however, is the objectivity of the narrative. It is hard to think of another work before the sixteenth century in which the author's guiding hand is so conspicuously absent, or which is so free from moral comment. For all the gaiety with which he treats sexual relationships, Martorell never allows his humour to soften the impact of what he is describing. His only concern seems to be to persuade the reader that this is how things must have happened, and it is for the reader himself to allocate praise and blame. Because it makes so few concessions to conventional morality, the *Tirant* is a disconcerting book, and this in itself is a sign of its vitality. In the end, however, it is the scope and depth of the vision which make it a masterpiece, a vivid and densely populated fictional world which still retains its power to convince.

VIII. MEDIEVAL DRAMA

Compared with the achievement in prose and poetry, the few surviving examples of medieval Catalan drama are slight and fragmentary, though here again there are interesting differences between Catalonia and the rest of the Peninsula. With very few exceptions, most Catalan plays before the nineteenth century are religious. There is evidence to show that some kind of liturgical drama in the vernacular existed at least from the fourteenth century onwards, centering, as one might expect, on the festivals of Christmas, Easter, and Corpus Christi. Moreover, it now seems clear that the early Latin liturgical drama entered Spain by way of Catalonia, and that it was basically a Catalan rather than a Castilian form. As R. B. Donovan has pointed out, this was partly the result of the liturgical situation itself: the fact that the Gallo-Roman rite established by Charlemagne spread to the newly founded Catalan monasteries, which for several centuries maintained their connection with the other side of the

Pyrenees.[67] (The most striking example of this is the close relationship which existed between Ripoll and Saint-Martial de Limoges, an association which is of unique importance in the early history of liturgical music and trope singing.)

The French influence can also be detected in matters of staging. Though it is almost impossible to decide the exact point at which mere pageant or recitation gave rise to genuine dramatic representation, it appears that the multiple stage characteristic of the French mysteries had a greater effect in Catalonia, and particularly in Mallorca, than elsewhere in the Peninsula. To judge from the body of plays which has survived from the early fifteenth century, there seems reason to believe in the existence of a separate Mallorcan dramatic tradition which is only reflected sporadically on the mainland. In both Barcelona and Valencia, however, there is enough evidence to show that the Corpus pageants had developed into genuine mystery plays at least by the early sixteenth century, and that these continued to be performed until much later alongside the more recent *autos sacramentales*.[68] In the sixteenth, seventeenth, and eighteenth centuries, such plays of medieval origin did a great deal to maintain popular traditions in a period of decadence; moreover, though the texts which have been preserved are often simple to the point of crudity, modern productions have shown that, given an adequate setting and a talent for mime, the results can be surprisingly impressive.

Some of the simpler forms of dramatic representation, like the *Cant de la sibil.la* (mid-thirteenth century?) and the Mallorcan *consuetes*, are still performed in connection with particular church festivals.[69] Occasionally a text has survived in something like its original form, like the fragments of a fourteenth-century Passion or the fourteenth-century *Visitatio sepulcri* from Vic. The language of this last play, though still noticeably influenced by Provençal, is simple and vigorous, as at the point where the Jews address the Roman soldiers who have witnessed the Resurrection:

Com stats vosaltres, cavallers?
Marrits e tristz, com vos pres?
Par que bataya haiats haüda,
Mas que no la haiats vensuda.
Tots vos vahem spauorditz:
Are ges no paretz ardits.
Vosaltres tots tremolats.
Dietz que'us ha 'nderroquats.
Sabetz si es al monument Jesus?
Dietz ho, e leuats sus.[70]

This is an unusually authentic example from an area in which ambitious vernacular productions seem to have been performed at a relatively early date. More often than not, however, the surviving texts have been greatly modified in the course of time. Thus the most famous of all these plays, the *Misteri d'Elx* (Elche), still performed each year on 12 and 13 August, dates only from the early seventeenth century in its present form. Like other surviving texts from Valencia and Castellón, this play is intended for performance on the Feast of the Assumption, and makes use of two pieces of stage machinery, the *mangrana*, or gilded cloud, which opens to reveal the angel of the Assumption, and the *araceli*, an aerial platform by which actors may be lowered from Heaven to Earth and raised again in the course of the performance. The use of such devices in itself suggests the strong element of pageantry which is inseparable from these productions. Clearly, it would be wrong to judge the texts of such pieces from a strictly literary point of view: none of them pretends to be more than a libretto, and the test of their value lies in their ability to survive as examples of a genuine popular culture which is no less real at the present day than at the time they were first written down.

NOTES

1. One of the earliest non-literary texts, the *Homilies d'Organyà*, a collection of six short sermons dating from the first half of the twelfth century, bears a certain similarity to Provençal, but already shows some of the most characteristic features of standard Catalan.

2. After 1137, the counts of Barcelona are also kings of Aragon. The joint nomenclature is sometimes confusing; thus, Pere I is at the same time Pedro II of Aragon, and Alfons I is also Alfonso II in Aragonese terms. For these rulers and their namesakes I have used the titles which are normally given them by modern Catalan historians.

3. Catalan rights over territories in the south of France had greatly increased in the course of the twelfth century. In supporting the Albigensians, Pere I was defending his own vassals; as a result of his intervention, the counts of Toulouse, Foix, and Comminges swore allegiance to him, thus making him sovereign—for seven months—over the entire Midi.

4. W. J. Entwistle, *The Spanish language* (London, 1936), 84.

5. As against this, Catalan evolved its own distinctive series of diphthongs formed by combining a stressed vowel with *u*, e.g. CLAVUM⟩ *clau*, CADERE⟩ *caure*, BREVEM⟩ *breu*, VIDERE⟩ *veure*, NIDUM⟩ *niu*, OVUM⟩ *ou*.

6. Compare the treatment of the Latin past participle: CANTATUM⟩ Fr. *chanté*; Sp., Port. *cantado*; Ital. *cantato*; Prov., Cat. *cantat*.

7. 'Let no one who is not sad, or who has never known sadness, heed my verses'.

8. The *Ensenhamen* of Guerau de Cabrera (*c.* 1150), a verse inventory of the poetry which a *joglar* might be expected to know, lists four Provençal troubadours, including Jaufre Rudel and Marcabru, and a great many narrative poems of the Carolingian, Breton, and classical cycles. Guerau also makes an interesting distinction between poems which were sung and others which were simply recited, though he says nothing of the language problem.

9. Peter Dronke, *The medieval lyric* (London, 1968), 207.

10. 'for they sing *liridumvau*, dancing and playing prettily and lightly ... for they sing *liridumvar*, dancing and playing high and clear'.

11. 'I know that the soul of my Marquis of Mataplana is in the best part of Paradise, there where the good King of France is, near Roland; and there also are my minstrel from the Ripollès and my Sabata too, along with fair ladies, on a bed strewn with flowers, beside Oliver of Lausanne'.

12. 'Do not take a false husband, delicate Jana'.

13. 'By lying you flatter the rich, by lying you receive gifts which otherwise would not be given; you lie when you sing and tell tales, you lie by seeming to be happy when you are secretly angry ... You eat free, but one would think you were a heretic, for you must eat alone'.

14. 'If by putting words together the making of poetry is *joglaria*, the great king and I are *joglars* in the same way'.

15. 'From the songs of the birds which I have heard in the fields I have refined my tongue'.

16. 'I adorn and refine your knowledge all the more'.

17. 'For it often happens that the understanding grasps one thing and the word signifies another which is contrary to the truth perceived by the understanding'.

18. 'The more obscure the similitude, the higher the understanding of the intellect which penetrates it'.

19. The best short exposition of Llull's system is R. Pring-Mill's *El microcosmos lul.lià* (Palma de Mallorca, 1961). For Llull's *ars memoriae*, see Frances Yates, *The art of memory* (London, 1966), chapter VIII.

20. 'Raise your understanding and you will raise your love'.

21. 'The girl realised that Blanquerna had spoken those words to her because he himself had known the same temptation; and she praised and blessed God who had given Blanquerna such power against temptation'.

22. 'A maidservant came out of each of the houses, carrying to the church a cloak and a pair of overshoes for her master and mistress'.

23. 'The lover was walking through a city like a madman, singing of his beloved, and people asked him if he had lost his reason. He replied that his beloved had deprived him of his will and that he had surrendered his understanding to him; and thus he was left only with the memory with which he recalled his beloved'.

24. See R. Pring-Mill, 'Entorn de la unitat del *Libre d'Amich e Amat*', *ER*, X (1962), 33-61.

25. 'The lover so loved his beloved that he believed all that he had said to him, and so desired to understand it that he wished to understand all that was spoken of him by necessary reasons. And thus the love of the lover was between faith and intelligence'.

26. 'The art, Lord, of minstrelsy began as a means of praising and blessing thee; to that end were invented instruments and dances, lays and new types of music, so that man should delight in thee'.

27. In particular, it bears a close resemblance to an anonymous Catalan poem of the mid-thirteenth-century, 'Augats, seyós qui credets Dèu lo payre' ('Hearken, sirs, who believe in God the Father'). See the critical edition of this poem by R. Aramon i Serra in *Hispanic studies in honour of I. González Llubera* (Oxford, 1959), 11-40.

28. 'I am an old man, poor and despised. I have no living creature to help me and I have undertaken too great an enterprise. I have searched through a great part of the world and given many good examples: I am little known and loved'.

29. 'I wish to die in a sea of love'.

30. 'I had the monastery of Miramar given to the Friars Minor, so that they might preach among the Saracens. Between the vine and the fennel, love seized me and made me love God and remain torn between sighs and tears'.

31. 'like pearls in sand, or sparrows in a thorn bush, or doves in a forest, by reason of the multitude and power of their enemies'.

32. For a vivid and well-documented account of Ripoll as a cultural centre, see R. d'Abadal, *L'abat Oliba, Bisbe de Vic, i la seva època* (Barcelona, 1948).

33. 'And we left for Borriana. And when we came to strike camp, [we found that] a swallow had made its nest on the roof of our tent, and we gave orders not to take down the tent until it had gone away with its little ones, since it had placed its trust in us'.

34. 'At this we went to bed, and would not reveal the conversation to any of those who were with us. And though it was January, and bitter cold, we tossed and turned in bed more than a hundred times in the course of the night, and sweated as if we were in a bath'.

35. 'Now the book leaves off speaking [of this matter] and turns to speak [of another]'.

36. The whole question of the use of verse sources in the chronicles is complex and controversial. See, for example, F. Soldevila, *Les prosificacions en els primers capítols de la Crònica de Desclot* (Barcelona, 1958) and 'Un poema joglaresc sobre l'engendrament de Jaume I' in *Estudios dedicados a Menéndez Pidal*, VII (1957), 71-80; M. Montoliu, *Les quatre grans cròniques* (Barcelona, 1959), 28-40, 141-9.

37. 'riding alone, with his weapons slung behind him; and he was running with sweat and tanned by the sun and by the great heat'.

38. 'For I and others who were vanquished at that time lost a great part of our possessions; and we never went back to live there, but rather have gone through the world seeking counsel and meeting with great ills, hardships, and dangers, and the greater part of us have died in these wars of the House of Aragon'.

39. 'Muntaner, rise up and try to write a book about the great marvels you have seen'.

40. 'A short time afterwards, Prince Jaume reached Barcelona, much troubled by sickness. When we went out to receive him, coming back into the city, a man was performing tricks for entertainment, crossing from one side of the street to the other on a thin rope. And we said to him: "Brother, do you see this sport?" And he replied: "My Lord, I see nothing". And as soon as he arrived at his lodgings, he took to his bed and after a few days rendered up his soul to our Lord God'.

41. 'And they make the law into a spider's web, which can hold nothing strong, but only flies and other weak creatures'. The image is taken from Seneca, though the vividness of the language is Eiximenis's own.

42. See, for example, J. Vicens Vives, *Notícia de Catalunya* (Barcelona, 1954), 114-16.

43. At the other extreme, there is the strange figure of Anselm Turmeda (*c.* 1352-*post* 1423), a Franciscan who, as the result of a spiritual crisis, became a Muslim, though he continued to write as a Christian, notably in the *Disputa de l'ase* (1418), a small masterpiece of irony now lost in its original form.

44. 'I am a man like other men, and I must follow in their footsteps'.

45. 'You know very well that men believe many things which they cannot see. —Indeed, said I, but I think them not wise who indulge in such things. I believe what I see, and pay no attention to the rest'.

46. 'you will not tell me that the said Seneca is a prophet or one of the patriarchs, who speak in figures; rather will you find him in every part a philosopher, who bases his matter on judgement and natural reason'.

47. 'Alas! It would have been better for me to be married or to have had a gentle lover than to have been a nun'.

48. 'Beneath my brow [i.e., in my eyes] I bear your lovely image at which I rejoice night and day, for, by looking repeatedly on the lovely features of your face, they have imprinted themselves on me, so that their form will not vanish when I die, but when I leave this world for the last time, those who bear my body to the grave will see your signature upon my face'.

49. 'I am this man who is called Ausias March'.

50. 'Leaving aside the style of the troubadours, who, carried away by passion, exceed the truth ...'

51. 'you are no virgin, since God wished you to bear offspring'.

52. 'The sea will boil like a pot in the oven, changing its colour and natural state, and it will appear to hate anything which rests for a moment on its surface; fish great and small will rush to save themselves and will seek secret hiding places: fleeing from the sea where they were born and bred, they will leap on to dry land as a last resort'.

53. 'If it is so, cancel my spirit, let my being return to nothingness, the more so if she be in such a place for my sake: let me not suffer so great an anguish'.

54. 'Her life had not yet ended, when I saw her lie near to death, saying amid tears: "Please do not leave me, have pity on my pain" '.

55. 'Those from whom death has taken *la mullar aimia* will be able to judge part of my grief'.

56. 'I fear you more than I love you'.

57. Ausias March, *Antologia poètica*, ed. Joan Fuster (Barcelona, 1959), 35.

58. 'in all base actions, mine was a savage heart'.

59. 'They hanged one of them and flayed her alive, a great witch and poisoner. She used to come at night, unaccompanied, and would climb up alone and tear out the teeth and molars of hanged men on their tall gallows'.

60. 'The sun cries out weeping with black hair and all the heavens clothed in dark sackcloth accompany the lament of your tongue'.

61. See Martí de Riquer (ed.), *Lletres de batalla*, *ENC* (Barcelona, 1963), 2 vols.

62. 'My intention is to make a man of him, though I do not mean to give him my love, but to strive to make him noble and valiant by having him believe I love him'.

63. 'And you, who have done battle for worldly vanities, fight now against the devil in defence of your soul. Oh, wretched one! Do you not repent of the battles you have waged for the vanity of the world? You have killed men and sent their souls to Hell'.

64. See Frank Pierce, 'The role of sex in *Tirant lo blanc*', *ER*, X (1962), 291-300.

65. 'And on account of the great heat, for she had had the windows closed, she was half unlaced, revealing her breasts, like two apples of Paradise ... which allowed the eyes of Tirant to enter in such a way that from that moment onwards they could find no means of leaving, and they remained forever imprisoned in the power of one who was free, until the two of them were parted by death'.

66. For a brilliant discussion of Martorell's narrative technique, see Mario Vargas Llosa's introduction to the recent Spanish translation of *Tirant lo blanc* by J. F. Vidal Jové (Madrid, 1969).

67. R. B. Donovan, *The liturgical drama in Spain* (Toronto, 1958), 25-9. See also N. D. Shergold, *A history of the Spanish stage from medieval times until the end of the seventeenth century* (Oxford, 1967), chapters I-III.

68. See A. A. Parker, 'Notes on the religious drama in medieval Spain and the origins of the "Auto sacramental" ', *MLR*, XXX (1935), 170-82. Recent scholarship confirms Parker's view that the *auto sacramental* is a Castilian form, whereas the mysteries are Catalan, Valencian, or Mallorcan.

69. Modern theories concerning the song of the Sybil who prophesies the birth of Christ and its later development, the dialogue between the Sybil and the Emperor, are summarised by Donovan, op. cit., 165-71. The term

consueta originally refers to the *ordinarium* or manuscript which recorded the order and content of the various church ceremonies, though later it became identified with the plays themselves.

70. 'How is it with you, sirs, downcast and sad? What has happened to you? It seems that you have been in battle, but that you have not won. We see you all filled with terror: you seem to have no courage left. You are all trembling. Tell us, what has cast you down? Do you know if Jesus is in the tomb? Tell us, rise up'.

Chapter 2

DECADENCE AND ENLIGHTENMENT

QUESTIONS OF SURVIVAL AND LOSS are quite crucial to the next major phase of Catalan literature, which runs from about 1500 to the beginning of the nineteenth century. This period is usually known as the 'Decadence', and, however much one may want to qualify the term, one can hardly reject it altogether. From the death of Martorell to the second half of the nineteenth century, there are no major writers in Catalan and until about a hundred years before this, the literary scene is one of almost unrelieved mediocrity. The reasons for this are complex, but there are several important points to bear in mind: (i) the decline in literature is one of standards, not of quantity; (ii) this decline is specifically literary: other kinds of art, for example, painting and architecture, did not suffer to nearly the same extent, and the eighteenth century in particular produced a number of outstanding intellectuals who wrote in Castilian; (iii) the literary situation does not correspond in any precise way to the pattern of economic prosperity and decline; (iv) nor does it reflect a change in the status of the Catalan language: Catalan remains the official language of the country until 1714, and the teaching of Catalan in schools is not prohibited until 1768.

It is only when one considers the apparent abruptness of the literary decline that a different kind of factor begins to emerge. The fifteenth century, clearly, is a period of considerable achievement, but even here there are signs that the situation is changing for the worse. After 1412, the country is ruled by the Castilian dynasty of the Trastámaras: Castilian becomes the familiar language at the Court, and one sign of this is the number of writers in the second half of the fifteenth century who use both Castilian and Catalan. This situation is confirmed by the union of Castile and Aragon in 1474, and in the sixteenth century, the Court withdraws still further from the Aragonese territories. As a result, the Catalan aristocracy is attracted more and more to the Castilian-speaking Court, while the mercantile classes fail to create a genuine culture of their own. When one reflects that practically any writer of importance before 1500 was connected in some way with the Court, one sees how serious the consequences were for literature. With the disappearance of the chancellory, the chief source of literary criteria was also removed; the desertion of the nobility and a succession of Castilian viceroys helped to complete the process.

Yet this picture is not altogether accurate. For one thing, Valencia, where bilingualism had deeper roots, tended to pull away from the influence of Barcelona: apart from the satirical poets, who continue to flourish until the seventeenth century, Valencian writers after 1500 go over almost entirely to Castilian, often with notable results.[1] And this coincides with a certain disintegration of the Catalan language itself, so that the weakening of linguistic norms leads to an increasing fragmentation of dialects. Many sixteenth-century writers continue to defend the use of Catalan for literary purposes, though never very forcefully, and their efforts merely emphasise the lack of any major talent.

The second qualification is even more important: it should be clear that, in speaking of 'decadence', one is thinking of sophisticated writing. Popular poetry, by contrast, remained the one source of genuine vitality throughout the whole period, even though its full importance was not realised until the nineteenth century. Compared with popular poetry in Castilian, the records are fairly sparse: the splendid examples incorporated in the Catalan translation of the *Decameron* (1429) are exceptionally early survivals; the first serious transcriptions date from the sixteenth century, and several important collections of the time, like the *Cancionero de Uppsala* (1556) and the *Flor de enamor-*

ados (1562), contain versions of Catalan songs. As in other countries, popular songs were often glossed or imitated by well-known poets: at least one of the pieces in the *Flor de enamorados* is by the dramatist Juan de Timoneda, and this and several others appear in different versions by the Catalan poet Pere Serafí (*c.* 1505-67). Many of these poems are religious: several of the best Catalan Christmas carols, like 'Oh, oh, oh, gran meravella', date from the fifteenth and sixteenth centuries;[2] some of the *goigs*, or poems in praise of the Virgin, are at least as old as this, though their very individual rhythms have continued to attract serious poets up to the present day.[3]

The other great source of popular poetry is the ballad: unlike their Spanish counterparts, Catalan ballads were not seriously collected until the nineteenth century, though it is clear that many of those which survive were composed as early as the sixteenth. Though their history is often difficult to reconstruct, two things seem certain: they make little or no use of episodes from medieval Catalan history, and the majority show a strong French or Castilian influence. Nevertheless, some of the finest Catalan ballads, like the *Comte Arnau* and *La dama d'Aragó*, are almost certainly of native origin, and from the seventeenth century to the nineteenth ballad-making appears as a natural response to historical events, from the anti-Castilian Revolt of 1640 to the Napoleonic Wars.

The only kind of literature which continues to flourish after 1500, therefore, is precisely the one which does not depend on the existence of a Court or of a cultured middle class. When one turns to sophisticated writing, the situation is very different. To put it briefly, Catalan literature, which so successfully adapts itself to the early stages of the Renaissance in the fifteenth century, fails to keep pace with the full expansion of vernacular literatures in the sixteenth. What happens in poetry is symptomatic of the whole situation. In the sixteenth century, minor poets like Pere Serafí and Joan Pujol continue to write in the style of Ausias March, though with none of his subtlety. The influence of Petrarch and later Italian poets, on the other hand, fails to dominate the older Provençal tradition, and when it finally does so, in the next century, this is mainly through the conscious imitation of Castilian models. The better poets of the period, in fact, seem curiously divided: Pujol is also the author of an epic poem on the battle of Lepanto (1571); Serafí is not only an imitator of Ausias March, but also a composer of emblems and one of the more successful popularising poets of the time. The best example here is Vicenç Garcia, Rector of Vall-fogona (1579/82-1623), the most skilful sonnet-writer of his day, but also the author of a quantity of burlesque and obscene verse which has always tended to overshadow his more serious achievement. Within his limits, Vicenç Garcia is a talented satirist, with occasional undertones of melancholy. Nor can one blame him for imitating Góngora and Quevedo: far better models, certainly, than the tired conventions of the troubadours. His basic failure lies deeper than questions of derivativeness: what is so conspicuously lacking in his work is any sense of the real seriousness of poetry. And with this goes an inevitable coarsening of language: however much one sympathises with his attempt to enlarge the poetic vocabulary of his time, the fact is that his works are full of unassimilated Castilianisms and unnatural twists of syntax.[4]

The only seventeenth-century poet who seems aware of the need to restore the dignity of the Catalan language is Francesc Fontanella (1615-c. 1680/85), the author of a pastoral *comedia, Amor, firmesa i porfia,* in the manner of Calderón, which represents a serious, though unsuccessful, attempt to create a new type of Catalan theatre. As for prose, it is curious that one of the few books of any merit (Riquer calls it 'the most important prose work of the Decadence') should be a forgery: the *Libre dels feyts d'armes de Catalunya* published under the name of Bernat Boades, an early fifteenth-century rector of Blanes, but actually composed by a later historian from the same town, Fra Joan Gaspar Roig i Jalpí (1624-91). This work, which continued to deceive scholars until a quarter of a century ago, is written in a pastiche of fifteenth-century Catalan and presented with a background of circumstantial evidence which must have seemed very convincing at the time. The following, for example, is part of a description of Jaume I:

> Mas empero ell fo bon Rey qui regi lo seu Reyalme el comtat de Barcelona e tota la demes terra, e nauem molt bones ordonances que ell fae en Catalunya per lo bon regiment dels catalans, e fo molt bellicoros e guerrejador, e de la sua persona molt alt e molt dispost, e molt bell de cara e de cors, e de molt bona paraula, e casi be tostemps parlaua ab la nostra lengua catalana, car lauors aquesta era la mes polida en Spanya. E axi mateix fo molt saui e molt letrat, car ell per la sua gran virtut hauia depres en la sua puericia no tan solament saber manejar les armes, e tirar la ballesta, e jugar la lança, e be seruirsen de la scona o de la spasa, e de les altres armes, mas encara bones letres, e de la sagrada Scriptura, e daltres moltes coses bones, axi com sen pertanyia a un Rey Darago e comte de Barcelona ...[5]

The actual literary merits of the *Libre dels feyts* are modest but genuine: the whole point of the forgery, however, was to provide evidence of the past greatness of Catalonia at a time when the future of the country was in the balance after the War of Separation of 1640-51. And seen in this light, it takes its place in a debate which gathers momentum in the course of the eighteenth century and is eventually carried into the Romantic period.

With the eighteenth century, the whole tone of Catalan culture changes once the intellectual life of the country moves into the orbit of the Enlightenment. At first, the signs are unpromising: the reprisals taken against Catalonia after the War of the Spanish Succession (1700-14) threatened to abolish its national identity altogether: the suppression of the autonomous government and the existing Catalan universities, together with the restrictions on the use of the Catalan language imposed by the *Decreto de Nueva Planta* (1716), were severe blows to what cultural life remained. Yet, even before 1700, there are signs of a revival of interest in civic and political questions among the professional classes and, despite the very real obstacles of the early eighteenth century, the continuity of the movement is never really broken.

The beginnings of the Catalan Enlightenment are tentative and unspectacular: one can point, however, to the growing importance of the University of Valencia and its connections with the newly established University of Cervera, or to the work of individuals like the Valencian historiographer Jacint Segura (1668-1749?) and the scholar and lawyer Gregori Mayans i Síscar (1699-1782). Nor should one overestimate the fact that most of the ideological writing of the time is in Castilian: for the most part, the language seems to have been regarded merely as an instrument of communication, without any real political implications. It is more to the point to notice the way in which the general current of ideas seems to lead naturally to the kind of defence of the Catalan language one finds in the second half of the eighteenth century, culminating in the first modern Catalan grammar, the *Gramàtica i apologia de la llengua catalana* of Josep Pau Ballot (1815). After 1750, the growing concern with Catalan tradition is backed by the founding of new institutions: the *Real Academia de Buenas Letras* (1752), the *Junta de Comercio de Barcelona* (1758), and the *Academia de Ciencias* (1764). And above all, perhaps, one senses a new feeling of confidence in the commercial society of Barcelona, especially after the opening-up of trade with the South American colonies in 1778.

The impact of all this on the literature of the time is fairly oblique. As in the rest of the Peninsula, there is a strong contrast between the vitality of ideas and the relative mediocrity of imaginative writing. What is arguably the best prose of the time, the *Calaix de sastre* of Rafael d'Amat i Cortada, Baron of Maldà (1746-1818), remained unpublished for the best part of a century, and there is still no complete edition. These memoirs, which run to sixty volumes, covering the period 1769-1816, contain vivid and detailed descriptions of contemporary events and are a mine of information concerning the social life of the time. There is nothing very personal or introspective about them: the fact that they were written in Catalan merely suggests that their author was following an established tradition of humorous writing, and they appear to have been conceived mainly as a record of popular tastes and happenings. Whatever their aims, they show gifts of observation and narrative skill which, in a different age, might have been the makings of an excellent social novelist, but which, under the circumstances, probably reached only a very small circle of readers.

For the most part, imaginative writing in the eighteenth century means poetry. Apart from the mass of popular verse on political and historical themes, most serious poetry of the time follows the prevailing Spanish modes. In the second half of the century, the last traces of the Baroque disappear in a wave of neo-classicism. Most of this poetry is tedious and badly written, though occasionally, as in the verse tragedies of the Menorcan writer Joan Ramis (1746-1819), one finds something which can compare with the best European models of the time.[6] This neo-classical phase, however, is interrupted by the French Revolution and the Napoleonic Wars, and the serious literary revival of the 1820s and '30s takes place under the influence of Romanticism.

The transition from three centuries of decadence to the nineteenth-century revival was anything but abrupt, and it is now quite clear that, without the modest achievements of the eighteenth century, there would have been very little to follow on later. There are at least two ways of misconstruing the history of Catalan literature between 1500 and 1800: one is to ignore the existence of popular traditions altogether; the other is to suppose that the vitality of such traditions was sufficient in itself to ensure the renewal of literary values. What was needed, of course, was a serious awareness of these cultural resources, the grounds for which were prepared in the eighteenth century by a whole series of minor writers and scholars who could scarcely have realised how important their work was to be for the future of Catalan literature.

NOTES

1. In the sixteenth and early seventeenth centuries there is a whole school of Valencian dramatists which includes Juan de Timoneda (d. 1583), Rey de Artieda (1549?-1613?), Cristóbal de Virués (1550-1609), and Guillén de Castro (1569-1631). The only Barcelona writer of any consequence in this period is the poet Juan Boscán (1474?-1542).

2. This and a number of other carols were collected in the *Cançoneret Rovirosa* of 1507. See Josep Romeu, *Cançons nadalenques del segle XV*, ENC (Barcelona, 1949) and the same author's study, *Les nadales tradicionals, estudi i crestomatia* (Barcelona, 1952).

3. The traditional *goig* is composed in hexasyllabic quatrains, with alternate masculine and feminine rhymes, e.g.,

> Ab goig e ab alegria,
> Senyor, del naixement,
> lausem Santa Maria
> et Déus omnipotent.

('With joy and happiness, Lord, at your birth, we praise the Virgin Mary and Almighty God'.)

4. The opening quatrain of one of his best-known sonnets shows some of the difficulties:

> Ab una pinta de marfil polia
> sos cabells de finíssima atzabeja,
> a qui los d'or més fi tenen enveja,
> en un terrat la bella Flora un dia.

(Literally: 'One day, on a flat roof, Flora was polishing with a comb her hair of finest jet, of which that of finest gold is envious'.) Both situation and diction suggest a weak imitation of Góngora. Apart from an obvious Castilianism like 'atzabeja' (= 'azabache') and the clumsy repetition of 'finíssima —més fi', the third line is rhythmically very lame, and the hyperbaton of the fourth sounds much more forced in Catalan than it would in Spanish.

5. 'But he was a good King, who ruled his Kingdom well—the county of Barcelona and the rest of his lands—, and we have inherited from him excellent decrees which he made in Catalonia for the good government of the Catalans, and he was very bellicose and warlike, and very tall and well-disposed in his person, and very fair in face and body, and of excellent speech, and he spoke almost all the time in our Catalan tongue, for in those days it was the most elegant in the whole of Spain. And in the same way he was very wise and learned, for through his great virtue he had in his youth not only learned to manage weapons and to shoot the crossbow and fight with a lance, and to use the javelin or the sword and other arms, but had studied good books and the Holy Scriptures and other excellent things, as was fitting for a King of Aragon and Count of Barcelona ...'

6. The appearance of a figure like Ramis is a sign of the distinctive cultural situation which existed in Menorca during the eighteenth century. From 1713 to 1781, apart from a brief French occupation in the course of the Seven Years War (1756-63), the island was under British rule, and enjoyed a period of commercial prosperity in marked contrast to conditions on the mainland. One result of this was the rise of an enlightened and cosmopolitan middle class, interested in maintaining economic and cultural connections with England, France, and Italy. Ramis himself was one of the founders of the *Societat de Cultura de Maó* (Mahon) (1778-85), whose discussions ranged from archaeology and the natural sciences to the works of Addison, Voltaire, and Young. Once Menorca reverted to the Crown of Castile in 1783, this movement came to an end, and Ramis himself virtually ceased to write in Catalan.

Chapter 3

THE NINETEENTH CENTURY

I. THE EARLY ROMANTICS

IN TERMS OF ACTUAL ACHIEVEMENT, the revival of Catalan literature in the early nineteenth century owes almost everything to
the Romantic Movement. As early as the 1790s, in the pages of
the newly founded *Diario de Barcelona*, one finds a growing
interest in the remote and the exotic, and a little later, the
traditionalist reaction provoked by the Napoleonic Wars brings
with it a heightened sense of the national past which is easily
assimilated into the ideology of the time. None of this is very
consciously formulated before the 1820s: the first landmark is
the publication of a magazine, *El Europeo* (1823-24), whose con-
tributors describe themselves as an 'escuela romántico-espiritual-
ista'. Two of the editors of *El Europeo*, Bonaventura Carles
Aribau and Ramón López Soler, were eventually to become
leading figures in the *Renaixença*, as the literary movement came
to be known, the first as the writer of the first important Romantic poem in Catalan, and the second as the author of *Los bandos
de Castilla* (1830), a historical novel in the manner of Scott,
whose preface is one of the earliest manifestos of Catalan Romanticism. In spite of its short life, *El Europeo* reflects very accurately the major preoccupations of the moment: the aesthetics of
Friedrich Schlegel, the vogue of Mme de Staël and Chateau-
briand, the revaluation of Shakespeare, and, above all, the
achievement of Goethe, Schiller, Scott, and Manzoni. What was
lacking at this stage was any serious attempt to write in the
Catalan language, the whole status of which was to remain in
doubt for the next few decades. Because of this, the work of

those Catalan authors who continue to use Spanish is an important index to the sensibility of the time and occasionally, as in the poetry of Manuel de Cabanyes (1808-33) and Pau Piferrer (1818-48) or the historical novels of Cosca Vayo (1804?-?) and Juan Cortada (1805-68), it contains some of the most original writing of the period.[1]

The language problem is partly a matter of audience: it is significant that the first successful plays in Catalan were not staged until the 1860s and that the first nineteenth-century novels of any serious literary merit came even later. In the early years of the *Renaixença*, the only new works to achieve any kind of public success were the bilingual *sainetes* of Josep Robrenyo (*c.* 1780-1838), an actor-dramatist who, despite his lack of literary pretensions, deserves the credit for having created a genuinely popular theatre in touch with the events of the time.[2]

With this one exception, the literary revival is exclusively concerned with poetry, and with poetry of a fairly conservative kind. The iconoclastic, anti-bourgeois note which appears in the Romantic literature of other countries is almost entirely missing from the *Renaixença*. In the 1830s, there was at least the possibility of a more radical, socially orientated type of writing which for various reasons—lack of cohesion, loss of nerve, the exile or death of some of its leading advocates—failed to materialise. Both before and after this, the movement is dominated by middle-class ideals and by the nostalgic evocation of a partly legendary past. It is symptomatic, for instance, that so many Catalan poets and critics of the Romantic period should refer to their language as 'lemosí', with all the troubadour overtones that the word conveys, and that the symbol of their group spirit should be the restoration of the interrupted tradition of the *Jocs florals* in 1859.[3]

The first nineteenth-century Catalan poem of any importance, Aribau's ode, *La pàtria* (1833), owed its effect not only to its genuine literary merits, but also to the quite remarkable way in which it condensed the feelings of nostalgia towards the country and the language which run through a number of slightly earlier poems. Curiously enough, the motive behind the poem was purely circumstantial: Aribau was one of a number of writers who were invited to compose poems in various languages as a birthday tribute to the Madrid banker Gaspar de Remisa; the task of writing a poem in Catalan fell to Aribau, and the whole tone of his ode comes from his anxious attempt to compete with more securely established languages. There is no denying his success: the degree of linguistic refinement which he achieved is enough to make the poem a landmark, and its publication in the Barcelona literary magazine *El Vapor* must have persuaded many readers that it was still possible to express a common mood with dignity and restraint.[4]

Aribau's example was followed a few years later by Joaquim Rubió i Ors (1818-99), one of the outstanding scholars of the time. The poems published by Rubió under the pseudonym 'Lo Gaiter del Llobregat' represent a much more conscious attempt to re-establish the tradition of Catalan verse. The first nineteen of the poems were originally published in the *Diario de Barcelona* between 1839 and 1840, and later collected in two volumes (1841; 1858), which contain a total of sixty poems. Though one misses the energy of Aribau, one can still admire the tact and skill with which Rubió adapts the gentler type of Romantic theme to his own language while avoiding the kind of linguistic purity which would have made his poems inaccessible to a popular audience. Their initial success was exactly what Catalan poetry needed at this stage, and the prefaces to the two volumes of *Lo Gaiter* are an accurate measure of their effect at the time. In the first, Rubió proclaims the need to create a new literature which will reflect the spiritual independence of the Catalan people. At this point, he admits that he is an almost solitary figure; seventeen years later, in the second preface, he is able to refer to a whole series of new poets who are following his example.

Characteristically, a number of these poets, like Víctor Balaguer (1824-1901) and Manuel Milà i Fontanals (1818-84), are also scholars, whose serious interest in history and popular traditions makes itself felt in a great deal of the patriotic poetry of the period. The turning-point comes with the restoration of the *Jocs florals* in 1859: before this, it is difficult to speak of a school of Catalan poetry, but from now on, there is a much greater sense of collective enterprise, as well as an assured audience and easier means of communication. For all this, the *Jocs florals* had their drawbacks: the motto which summarised their aims—'Pàtria, Fe, Amor'—encouraged countless untalented poets to express themselves in naïve and conventional terms and, at their worst, they merely confirmed and exaggerated the basic conservatism of the *Renaixença*. Yet their historical importance is beyond question: without them, it would probably have taken much longer for the new poetry to find an audience and, above all, they provided a starting-point for those writers of the next generation—Verdaguer, Oller, and Guimerà—whose work was to render their further existence superfluous.

II. VERDAGUER

At the *Jocs florals* of 1877, the first prize was awarded to an epic poem in ten cantos, the *Atlàntida* of Jacint Verdaguer (1845-1902). Nothing could have prepared the audience for a poem of such scope and originality, and its reception immediately established its author as the first major Catalan poet of the nineteenth century. Verdaguer at the time was a young priest with country roots who, because of ill-health, had spent several years as chaplain to a transatlantic shipping company, an experience which had encouraged him to complete a long poem on the destruction of Atlantis begun some years earlier and set aside. After this initial success, he wrote a second epic, *Canigó* (1885), as well as a number of other long poems and collections of lyrics. His later years were clouded by scandal: an over-zealous interest in exorcism and extravagant acts of charity which involved him in serious debt brought him into conflict with the ecclesiastical authorities, and for a time he was suspended from his duties as a priest. None of this, however, affects the achievement of his poetry or the esteem in which he was held by his contemporaries, and the whole episode points more to the basic simplicity of Verdaguer's temperament than to any lack of religious vocation.

Seen at this distance, the attempt to write epic poetry in the second half of the nineteenth century may seem naïve and anachronistic. Certainly it suggests Verdaguer's isolation as a poet, though paradoxically it was this isolation which enabled him to rise above the existing poetic tradition. At the same time, neither the *Atlàntida* nor *Canigó* is in any sense an academic poem, and what saves them is the sheer energy of their vision and the language which matches it. This is not to deny their debts to other writers: the sources of the *Atlàntida*, for example, include Plato, Nieremberg, the early chroniclers of America, and several nineteenth-century naturalists and explorers. What is surprising is the assurance with which Verdaguer knits his materials into an intensely personal rendering of the basic myth. In the final version of the poem, the story of Hercules and the destruction of Atlantis is told to the young Columbus, so that the discovery of the New World appears to restore the cosmic unity which was broken by the legendary disaster. Read purely as a narrative, the poem has its faults: its protagonists—Hercules, Hesperis, and Columbus—are insufficiently characterised, and the Columbus episode is joined awkwardly to the central myth. But the real unity of the poem, one can argue, lies deeper: in a sense, its underlying theme is power, and Verdaguer's Romantic affinities are nowhere so clear as in his attempt to fuse the pagan and Christian worlds in a pattern of cosmic retribution and renewal. The most memorable passages of the *Atlàntida* are those which describe the fate of the corrupt yet beautiful civilisation of Atlantis:

> Mes ja, pels llamps i onades arrabassats, sortien
> de Calpe els esgardissos i arrels a l'ample espai
> en daus cairuts i pannes que sa buidor omplien,
> l'hermosa llum a veure que no vegeren mai.

I esgarrifats del caos, s'engorguen altra volta
damunt carreus que els feien ahir de fonament,
i els antres tenebrosos d'aquella mar revolta
retronen i s'escruixen al gran capgirament.

De les gentils Hespèrides lo tàlem s'aclofava,
llurs cims, desarrelant-se, s'asseuen en les valls,
i en aücs horrorosos i gemegô esclatava,
com dona que en mal part llança els darrers badalls.[5]

Such a passage conveys very powerfully the ugliness and terror which are part of the spectacle of human weakness. This is to some extent a matter of language: images like 'el sol caduc, a palpes buscant sos cabells rossos',[6] or 'cremant com teranyines els núvols de l'hivern',[7] have a visionary sweep which at the same time is rooted in direct observation. The driving force behind them comes from a clear-cut sense of good and evil in which there is no place for ironies or ambiguities; again, the kind of effect which would hardly be possible in a more sophisticated writer, yet is one of the surest signs of Verdaguer's integrity as a poet.

Canigó, his second epic, is closer to the preoccupations of earlier Romantic writers in that it deals with the legendary origins of Catalonia. Again, there is a direct confrontation of pagan and Christian themes: the folk-tale atmosphere which surrounds the enchantment of a young Christian knight by the mountain spirits of the Pyrenees is set against the background of the Moorish invasion of Roussillon, and the final defeat of the pagan spirits is symbolised by the founding of the Benedictine monastery of Sant Martí del Canigó. Part of Verdaguer's intention, clearly, was to convey the workings of Providence in the formation of the Catalan national consciousness. The epic dimension of the poem comes from his deliberate attempt to re-create the spirit of the *chansons de geste*; compared with the *Atlàntida*, however, much more importance is given to the lyrical episodes and to the re-working of popular poems and legends. This makes for a degree of intimacy which is unusual in a poem of this scope: Verdaguer's heroes are continually seen in the act of contemplating a landscape which, despite its almost mystical significance, bears a dense weight of local associations and specific detail:

> A l'arribar al caire de la serra,
> de Guifre i sos guerrers ell se recorda.
> Gira ab recança la mirada enrera;
> lo Rosselló a sos ulls que bell se mostra
> voltat d'una filera d'alimares
> que d'una a una en cada cim se posen!
> En cada cap de puig dels que rodegen
> la plana de Ruscino, hi ha una torre,
> una torre gentil que al cel arriba
> per abastar l'estrella ab què s'enjoia.[8]

Because of this, *Canigó* is a more immediate poem than the *Atlàntida*, and the actions of the human characters are interwoven with the processes of an intensely animated landscape. In a sense, the Pyrenees themselves are the real protagonists of the poem, and it is they who embody the conflict between the symbolic world of Christianity and the densely populated nature of pagan myth. Artistically, the richness of the poem depends on its being able to make the most of both worlds: the sense of national purpose and epic severity which come with the triumph of Christianity impose themselves on the disordered beauty of the pagan supernatural, but only after this has provided the poem with its most luxuriant descriptions.

Between them, *Canigó* and the *Atlàntida* represent the height of Verdaguer's achievement in the long poem. The range of their language and vocabulary are unequalled in later Catalan poetry, and their appearance in the last quarter of the nineteenth century established beyond any doubt the possibilities of Catalan as a modern literary language. Verdaguer's shorter poems, which run into several hundreds, are more closely linked to his religious vocation. A great many of them fall into the category of unpretentious and undemanding devotional verse, yet even at his most conventional, Verdaguer writes out of a sure sense of the values and language of popular poetry. His best collections of lyrics, like *Flors del Calvari* (1896) and *Aires del Montseny* (1901), are more original. The first of these contains the poems written in the course of his difficulties with the Church; in the second, which seems to look back elegiacally over the whole of his past experience, he achieves a conversational tone which is unlike anything in his earlier verse. It is difficult to generalise about such a large and varied body of work. A great deal has been written about Verdaguer's mysticism, though this hardly seems the right word to describe a poetry which dwells so consistently on the beauty of the natural world. What binds together both the popular and religious strains in his verse is the kind of Franciscan simplicity, verging at times on gaiety, which one finds in these verses from *Aires del Montseny*:

> M'estic a l'hostal
> de la Providència,
> servit com un rei
> per mà de la reina.
> Ella em dóna el vi
> de la vinya seva:
> ella em dóna el pa,
> me'l dóna i me'l llesca.[9]

The final image could hardly be simpler, yet, as Carles Riba has noted,[10] the verb 'llesca' brings with it a sense of the whole context of daily living. This, one may feel, is traditional writing in the best sense, in that it draws on a range of experience which inheres in the words themselves, and Verdaguer is the first poet in modern times to be fully aware of the communal resources of the Catalan language.

III. NARCÍS OLLER

The successes of the *Renaixença* were almost entirely confined to poetry. In their early years, the *Jocs florals* did a certain amount to encourage prose-writing, but it is doubtful whether on their own they could have created the kind of novel-reading public which is so clearly lacking before the 1870s. Predictably, the majority of mid-nineteenth-century fiction belongs to the *costumbrista* school, whose most talented representative in Catalonia is Emili Vilanova (1840-1905).[11] What was badly needed at this stage was a writer capable of making the transition from the small-scale *quadre de costums* to the full-length novel of society. In Spain, this transition had already been achieved by Galdós and other novelists; in Catalonia, the crucial moment came with the emergence of a complex and distinctive Restoration society which felt itself, however superficially, to be part of the European scene.

It is this European quality which strikes one in the work of Narcís Oller (1845-1930), the one really gifted Catalan novelist of the late nineteenth century. One of Oller's greatest achievements is to have created a public for a type of novel which reflects the most serious tendencies of contemporary realism. His own early career illustrates some of the difficulties involved: like other writers of his generation, he began to write in Castilian, and it was only after attending the *Jocs florals* of 1877—the occasion on which Verdaguer first read his *Atlàntida*—that he seems to have been convinced of the value of Catalan as a literary medium. Two years later, he published his first collection of stories, *Croquis del natural*, and in 1882, the first of his four novels, *La papallona*, established him as the leading prose-writer of the day.

Despite this success, Oller never regarded himself as a professional man of letters. His early years were spent in Valls (Tarragona), a provincial background which he used to great effect in his second novel, *Vilaniu* (1885). His closest friend at this stage was his cousin, Josep Yxart (1852-95), eventually to become one of the best critics of his generation, and one of the people whom Oller introduced into Barcelona literary society after he had permanently settled there in the early 1870s.[12] The later part of Oller's career was uneventful. Except for occasional visits to Paris, he continued to work as a lawyer until almost the end of his life: his last novel, *Pilar Prim*, was published in 1906; his literary memoirs, *Memòries literàries: història dels meus llibres*, break off at this same year and, apart from a few fragments, were only published for the first time in 1962.

Behind Oller's final silence there lies an awareness of a changing artistic climate in which there no longer seemed to be a place for his own kind of fiction. As he writes in *Memòries literàries*: 'L'alba del segle XX m'atrapà en un estat de depressió moral terrible', and, after referring to the deaths of Yxart and Sardà, he goes on:

> sentint-me absolutament refractari a les temes i tendències que anaven dibuixant-se en el nou art batejat llavors de modernisme, m'entrà un descoratjament i tot ensems un fàstic tan gran per a seguir conreuant les lletres.[13]

As we shall see, it was not only *modernisme* which ran counter to Oller's concept of the novel: the movement known as *noucentisme* which succeeded it virtually ignored Oller's achievement, in favour of a narrowly aesthetic approach to fiction.

Though his production is relatively small, there is an air of inevitability about Oller's novels which corresponds to the major phases of his own career. Thus, *La papallona* reflects his life as a student, *Vilaniu* the early background of Valls, *La febre d'or* his professional life in Barcelona, and *Pilar Prim* the complex vision of the experienced writer. It was to be expected that some of Oller's early critics should refer to him as a Naturalist, though Zola's own preface to the French translation of *La papallona* was more perceptive. Speaking of Oller's gift for seeing things 'à travers un talent attendri', he observes that 'Barcelone s'agite dans les descriptions avec une réalité intense, tandis que les personnages marchent un peu au-dessus de la terre'. Oller's own comment on first reading Zola is also significant: it revealed to him, he says 'el gran contingut de poesia que conté a voltes el natural per qui sap observar-lo'.[14]

Taken together, these remarks point to the strong current of Romantic idealism which runs through all Oller's work. Compared with Zola himself, he is more interested in individuals and much less in generalisations about society. Nothing could be further from Oller than Zola's peculiar kind of determinism: his marvellous sense of detail is never allowed to obscure the development of the plot. With the exception of *Pilar Prim*, all Oller's novels are *romans à thèse*, in which the triumph of moral justice tends to be achieved against the grain of events. This is particularly true of an early work like *La papallona*; in *Vilaniu*, the problem is more complex, in so far as the social milieu is more finely observed. Even so, it comes as no surprise to find that the more personal parts of the novel are based on an earlier story, *Isabel de Galceran*, which in turn reflects a sentimental episode from the author's own youth. Because of this, the accurate presentation of provincial society is at odds with the romantically idealised intrigue, and this conflict tends to undermine the realistic intentions of the whole. Oller, always his own best critic, seems to have realised at the time that he was attempting the impossible, and in his third novel, *La febre d'or* (1890-93), confined himself strictly to the observation of contemporary life. In some ways, this is his masterpiece: as a picture of a society obsessed by financial speculation it could hardly be surpassed, and its documentary accuracy is completely convincing. Yet even here, there is a central flaw, in that the basic plot—the story of the financial rise and fall of a single family—is hardly strong enough to convey the full dimensions of the social drama. The final twist in the fortunes of the protagonist, Gil Foix, is touching and pathetic at a personal level, but takes place at several removes from the society which is so brilliantly analysed in the rest of the novel. What is lacking, ultimately, is a strength of characterisation which would focus and dominate the realistic observation of a whole community.

In his last important works of fiction, the long story *La bogeria* (1899) and the novel *Pilar Prim* (1906), Oller seems consciously to depart from the realistic formula of his earlier novels. Looking back on this period in his memoirs, he is aware that a new generation of novelists with more literary intentions is beginning to compete with his own, less reflective, kind of realism. Touchingly, and without the least sense of irony, he compares himself, not to the professionals like Daudet and Zola, but to another amateur novelist—Stendhal. Yet, just before his final silence, Oller seems to be on the verge of creating a distinctly more modern type of fiction. *La bogeria* traces the mental development of a psychopath through the memories of a first-person narrator, and in *Pilar Prim*, the most subtle of his novels, the entire plot is centred on the reactions of the characters themselves, to the almost total exclusion of naturalistic observation. The young widow of the title is the victim both of her husband's will and of a hostile society which condemns her emotional involvement with a younger man. Unlike Oller's other novels, *Pilar Prim* contains no moral: instead, he implies that, however much the heroine is dishonoured socially, she will be saved from moral degradation by the integrity of her own feelings. The conclusion of *La bogeria* had been pessimistic: in the asylum, as in life itself, 'L'ordre, el regalament, una habitud ordinària, el lucre, hi ofegaran el sentiment'.[15] In his last novel, Oller seems to qualify this and to suggest, what the more romantic side of his nature appears always to have believed, that the true measure of an individual lies in his feelings, and that these will always be the ultimate guarantee of his authenticity.

IV. GUIMERÀ

The late 1870s are also crucial years in the history of the Catalan theatre. In the first half of the century, full-length plays in Catalan are non-existent: the typical productions of the time, both amateur and professional, continue the eighteenth-century tradition of the *sainete*, though occasionally, as in the work of Josep Robrenyo (discussed above, p. 71), there is a genuine attempt at a popular political theatre. Many of these short plays are bilingual: following the tradition, the most popular dramatist of the 1860s, Frederic Soler ('Serafí Pitarra'; 1839-95), defended the use of 'el català que ara es parla' ('Catalan as it is now spoken'), meaning by this the language of the lower classes of Barcelona. The limitations of such a criterion were severe, and, though many of the plays of this type are of great documentary interest, their literary value is negligible. At the very least, however, they kept the theatre alive through a difficult period, and the tradition of acting and production which grew up round them remained one of the great strengths of the late nineteenth-century drama.

Whatever its actual quality, the Catalan theatre of the time reflects very accurately the growing affluence of the urban middle classes. In 1865, the first full-length play in Catalan— *Tal faràs, tal trobaràs*, by Eduard Vidal i Valenciano—was produced in Barcelona, and from that point onwards, the middle-class social drama tends to overshadow the more popular *sainete*. This cleavage appears very simply in the career of Soler, who, after establishing himself as the most popular dramatist of the time, followed the example of Vidal and turned over completely to the conventional thesis play.

The first attempts to raise the literary status of the theatre came from a very different direction: the Romantic historical drama. The pioneer here is the poet and historian Víctor Balaguer (see above, p. 72), whose tragedies, particularly those on Catalan themes, are a serious effort to bridge the gap between the theatre and the world of the *Jocs florals*. As plays, they are hardly more than sequences of dramatic monologues spread over a mimimal plot; historically, however, they are the only precedents in Catalan for the infinitely more ambitious dramas of Guimerà.

Àngel Guimerà (1845-1924) is the one nineteenth-century Catalan dramatist of European stature. His early poems, like *L'any mil* (1877), already show a Romantic sense of history and an objective vision which seem made for the stage. His first plays, *Gala Placídia* (1879) and *Judit de Welp* (1883), are

historical verse dramas in the grand manner—the manner of
Victor Hugo and the Spanish Romantics. Even granting a certain
derivativeness, their importance in the theatrical context of the
time is enormous, and their blank verse has a spaciousness and
thrust which leave one in no doubt that a new dramatic language
is being created. As for their subjects, perhaps only a writer with
Guimerà's unqualified faith in Romantic values would have been
capable of working effectively within such terms. The best of his
verse plays, *Mar i cel* (1888), has most of the ingredients of a
Verdi opera: a young girl destined for a convent, captured on
the high seas by a corsair of Othello-like nobility with whom she
reluctantly falls in love, and with whom she finally dies at the
hands of her sternly repressive father. An absurdly melodramatic
plot: yet what gives the play its authority is Guimerà's superb
sense of timing, the way in which his verse never fails to rise to
a dramatic climax, and the use of creative metaphor which makes
the language worth dwelling on for its own sake, as when Blanca,
the heroine, reflects on her sheltered childhood:

> I al mur hi vaig pujar des d'una soca.
> Quin goig, mon Déu! ... a l'altra part tot eren
> carrers i gent; a sota meu jugaven
> dos nens rossos com l'or; quanta ventura
> en son riure i saltar! Mes, d'una porta
> una dona sortí: fills meus, que arriba
> vostre pare, els va dir, quan ja els alçava
> en sos braços un home ... tan feréstec
> com aquestos ho son, i jo sentia
> ses paraules i besos amorosos...
> i plorava com ell; perquè ell plorava!
> Tot això va passar; coses de nena!
> Ja gran, després, tan sols en la clausura
> he desitjat lo goig d'aquí a la Terra.
> Mes, jo em pregunto avui: què has fet, oh dona,
> per ton Déu i Senyor?...[16]

Mar i cel is the last of the verse dramas, and already there are moments when the pressure of the dialogue seems to be forcing it towards prose. Guimerà's next play, *La boja* (1890), marked the beginning of a new phase in his work, one which was to include his two masterpieces, *Maria Rosa* (1894) and *Terra baixa* (1897). This phase has often been called 'naturalistic', and, on the surface at least, the contrast with the earlier plays is very striking. If *Mar i cel* suggests Verdi, the theme of *Maria Rosa*—the consequences of a vulgar crime among a group of roadworkers—might have appealed to Hauptmann or Brecht. These rural dramas clearly owe a great deal to direct observation, and the language of the characters is based on an accurate knowledge of provincial speech. If the question of Naturalism arises, it is precisely because of this absolute authenticity of setting and dialogue. Yet, in a sense, these are the most poetic of all Guimerà's plays, and the reason lies partly in their intention. The real power of both *Maria Rosa* and *Terra baixa* comes, not from their realism, but from a simple mythical pattern which is embodied in the lives of their chief protagonists. Both Maria Rosa and Manelic, the shepherd who is the hero of *Terra baixa*, are simple and passionate individuals who are made to suffer cruelly by a cynical piece of deception. Maria Rosa's husband dies in prison after being sentenced for a murder he never committed, and the real criminal attempts to take his place in her life; Manelic is deceived into marrying Marta, the mistress of the local *cacique*, so that the latter's own marriage may take place without scandal. In each instance, the potential victim escapes from the net in a violent and magnificent gesture of self-assertion, though in *Terra baixa* the break is made much more cleanly than in the earlier play. Cleanly, that is to say, in an idealistic sense: as the play ends, Manelic, having killed the villainous *cacique*, makes for the mountains with Marta in his arms. On the stage, the intensity of this final moment is so great that one hardly pauses to think what the solution in real life might be: a simple and satisfying pattern is completed, and Guimerà's skill is such that he makes it appear to rise quite naturally from the realistic circumstances of the play. Because of this, *Terra baixa* is hardly the genuine tragedy it is sometimes made out to be: Manelic is potentially tragic in that he is an innocent and simple-hearted person who is compelled to recognise the existence of corruption, but it would take a more consistently realistic play, one feels, in order to sustain the tragedy. This is not so much a criticism of the play as an indication that its real interest lies elsewhere: in the pathos of a genuinely good individual who is made to realise that his marriage is based on a lie, yet is able to win his wife's affections by his simple authority.

Guimerà's later plays are more consciously symbolic and generally less convincing than the rural dramas. His most memorable effects are invariably linked to his mastery of the common language, and a play like *La reina jove* (1911), despite some powerful moments, really demands a sophisticated, Shavian type of dialogue which is outside his range. This play and others of his final period also tend to suffer from sentimentality, from a kind of social naïveness which is probably central to Guimerà, but which only becomes obtrusive in an urbane setting. These later plays are more openly didactic than the others, and usually in a social sense. And, though the genuineness of Guimerà's social conscience is never in doubt, the evangelical good faith which gave strength to his earlier work often makes his handling of political themes seem merely Ruritanian. Even his weaker plays, however, show a kind of large-scale craftsmanship which was unknown in the Catalan theatre before his time and which has seldom been equalled since. Perhaps this was inevitable: Guimerà's great gifts were basically those of a Romantic artist, and it says a great deal for the integrity of his talent that he was able to translate the power of his original vision into an impressive variety of plays until well after the turn of the century.

V. MODERNISME; THE POETRY OF MARAGALL

With Verdaguer, Oller, and Guimerà, the *Renaixença* as a serious movement came to an end: each of these writers, by the sheer force of his talent, had extended the range of literary Catalan beyond anything which could have been conceived in the 1860s. From this moment onwards, one can detect a new sense of urgency in the literary situation and, by the closing years of the nineteenth century, the European qualities which already appear in the novels of Oller have spread to the other sectors of literature and the arts. This new sensibility of the 1890s came quickly to be known as *modernisme* or, alternatively, *decadentisme*, though neither term was very clearly defined. The poet Joan Maragall (1860-1911), in many ways the most clear-sighted critic of the movement, saw it as a re-emergence of the Romantic spirit after the interlude of Naturalism. Other statements of the time, like those of Soler i Miquel, confirm what was probably the greatest strength of *modernisme*, its renewed confidence in the value of artistic intuition.[17] Though their Romantic affinities are clear enough, one can gauge the novelty of the *modernistes* simply by listing the foreign writers who most interested them: Carlyle, Ruskin, Nietzsche, Ibsen, and Maeterlinck. As might be expected, these influences affected not only literature: the vogue of Maeterlinck, in particular, was used to justify the association of poetry and drama with the other arts, and both the painting and the architecture of the time reflect the peculiar medievalism of the Pre-Raphaelites.[18]

It is Maragall's relations with *modernisme* which show most clearly the strengths and weaknesses of the movement. As a young man, Maragall had grown up into the Restoration society described in the novels of Oller. In his *Notes autobiogràfiques* of 1885-86, he discusses his misgivings at having embarked on a still uncertain literary career. By 1891, he had begun to make a name as a poet: the tenacity of purpose one senses in the *Notes* had been strengthened by a happy marriage and by friendships with several important writers, among them Yxart and Oller. Also, in one decisive aspect, his literary tastes were already formed: his translation of Goethe's *Römische Elegien* (1888), which seems to have had a liberating effect on the tone and rhythms of his own verse, had been one of the first results of his lifelong devotion to the German writer, an influence which, at least in his early years, was as much moral as literary.

This sense of affinity with an older writer is one sign of the independence of mind which was to make Maragall the best critic of his generation. In 1890, he joined the staff of the *Diario de Barcelona* as private secretary to the editor, Mañé i Flaquer, a post which he held until 1903. As a journalist, Maragall not only wrote extensively on political and social questions but also reviewed many of the most characteristic productions of the *modernistes*. Much of the interest of his criticism comes from the degree of sympathy he feels for the movement as a whole: his enthusiasm for Ibsen and Maeterlinck is unmistakable, and his reading of Nietzsche marked the beginning of a debate which profoundly influenced some of his later poems. Yet, with a few minor exceptions the poetry which Maragall wrote at the time is scarcely affected by the prevailing mood, and before long he begins to criticise contemporary literary fashions. In Ibsen and Maeterlinck, for example, he finds on the one hand a rigidity of theme and on the other an excess of sensibility which in both instances leads to a fragmentary vision of life. But it is above all in his criticisms of the plays and stories of Santiago Rusiñol (1861-1931), the leading *modernista* writer and painter,[19] that he is able to point to the basic weakness of the whole movement:

La tristeza [he wrote in 1900] parece ser el resorte estético de nuestro poeta-pintor; el humorismo, la *blague*, tan característico de su personalidad en muchas de sus obras, se nos figura como simple distensión de unos nervios que han vibrado demasiado en la belleza de las cosas tristes ...[20]

These critical pieces of the 1890s are an important stage in Maragall's education as a poet: in diagnosing the lack of vitality in a movement which nevertheless attracted him, he is feeling his way towards the conception of artistic wholeness which underlies the far greater achievement of his own later poems.

Maragall's poems are contained in five volumes: *Poesies*

(1895), *Visions i cants* (1900), *Les disperses* (1903), *Enllà* (1906), and *Seqüències* (1911). His early verse is mainly personal, though in some of the poems on natural themes (*Goigs a la Verge de Núria, La vaca cega*) the balance between inwardness and objectivity already conveys the sense of nature as a source of energy and spiritual renewal which runs through his later work. And in one poem in particular, *Paternal* (1893), written after an anarchist bomb outrage, the idealistic anarchism which he had admired in Nietzsche is confronted with its practical implications in a synthesis which affects both public and private life. The anecdote on which the poem is based is strikingly simple : the poet, shocked by the event he has just witnessed, returns home to find his wife feeding their young child :

> A cada esclat mortal—la gent trèmula es gira :
> la crudeltat que avança—la por que s'enretira,
> se van partint el món ...
> mirant el fill que mama,—la mare que sospira,
> el pare arruga el front.[21]

The obvious contrast between public violence and domestic peace is deceptive. In the last line of the poem, the satisfied child 'laughs barbarously' ('riu bàrbarament'), and the phrase echoes the words which Maragall had used a few years before to express his enthusiasm for the ideas of Nietzsche : 'una refrescadora vuelta a las grandes sinceridades de la barbarie'.[22] In the poem, as in his letters of the time, Maragall is clearly horrified by the practical consequences of an attitude which he had once approved. As he presents it, the collective tragedy is 'barbarous' only in a negative sense : yet against its futile destructiveness there is only Nietzsche's own vision of the child as the supreme creator of new values : 'The child is innocence and forgetfulness, a new beginning, a sport, a self-propelling wheel, a first motion, a sacred affirmation' (*Also sprach Zarathustra*, 'Of the three metamorphoses'). Maragall himself had translated this passage, and it seems likely that he remembered it at what was a crucial moment for his own beliefs. So in his poem, he strikes a precarious balance between the two kinds of barbarism by suggesting the unconscious optimism of the child, while condemning the sterility of the public act.

By 1900, Maragall had rejected Nietzsche, though one part of his imagination continued to dwell on themes of violence and heroism. As he wrote in 1902 to Pere Coromines:

> La lluita repugna a la meva naturalesa que en tot cerca un centre d'harmonia i serenitat, però els lluitadors m'interessen fortament perquè frueixen de la vida un aspecte que m'és desconegut.[23]

Two years before this, he had published *Visions*, a group of poems on Catalan legends and folk-heroes, 'figures de personajes legendarios catalanes tales cuales puede verlos un poeta de hoy' (letter to Felip Pedrell, 9 January 1900). The last phrase is revealing: Maragall was aware that he was dealing with figures— Joan Garí, the seventeenth-century bandit Serrallonga—who had already attracted earlier poets, including Verdaguer; at the same time, he sees them as a means of exploring the ambivalent feelings about the nature of power which occur in some of his poems and essays of the 1890s.

One of the poems of *Visions*, *El comte Arnau*, continued to engage his imagination for the next ten years: encouraged by the composer Pedrell, who set the early sections of the poem to music, Maragall went on to write two further parts, the last of which was published in 1911, a few months before his death.[24] His apparently casual method of composition—he himself admitted that the full sense of the *Comte Arnau* sequence did not come to him until after it was completed—is based on the faith in the power of intuition which he discusses in *Elogi de la paraula* (1903), his Presidential address to the *Ateneu Barcelonès*, and, more subtly, in the *Elogi de la poesia* (1907). In these and other prose pieces of the same period, Maragall is concerned, not so much with criticism, as with redefining certain key terms— 'word', 'song', 'inspiration', 'people'—which he feels are in danger of becoming clichés. This attempt, which places him in the tradition of Carlyle, Emerson, Matthew Arnold, and other nine-teenth-century poet-thinkers, is a more conscious application of the organic principle which appears to lie behind his longer poems. Maragall's whole view of poetry emphasises the frag-mentary nature of poetic inspiration and the idea that the con-tent of a poem should be dictated by what he calls 'rhythm':

> La força del ritme li duu paraules i sols després veu vostè el pensament que li porten: és la revelació per la forma.[25]

Such ideas explain Maragall's reluctance to *construct* a long poem, and also the fact that his most ambitious poems—the three parts of *El comte Arnau* and the *Haidé* sequence—are really accumulations of shorter poems, held together by a number of recurring concepts. In Maragall's later work, these concepts come to centre around the twin themes of renunciation and redemp-tion. So, in the final part of *El comte Arnau*, it is quite literally the power of poetry which redeems the legendary protagonist from the damnation he is made to suffer in the folk-ballad, and in the *Haidé* poems, human love becomes a metaphor for divine grace.

These, of course, are Romantic solutions: the striking thing is the way in which their basic assumptions seem rooted in the whole of Maragall's later experience. In 1911, after completing *El comte Arnau*, he wrote:

> Jo no puc concebre l'altra vida deslligada d'aquesta ... El fer de la vida humana, terrena i ultraterrena, una sola cosa, ve-li aquí el sentit més personal meu del poema, que no és sinó la preocupació fonamental de la meva vida.[26]

This is the basic meaning, not only of the *Cant espiritual* (1910), Maragall's most searching meditation on death, but also of one of his finest articles on a civic theme, *La iglésia cremada*, in which he attempts to come to terms with the anarchist rising of the *Semana trágica* (1909).[27] In all these writings, and in his last major work, the verse play *Nausica* (1908-10), Maragall's thoughts seem to centre on the redeeming power of suffering.

And in *Nausica*, based on Goethe's abandoned project for a tragedy on the episode from the *Odyssey*, it is the heroine herself who is made to suffer by the strength of her feelings, but who, through her renunciation of Ulysses, achieves a nobler conception of love in which memory becomes a permanent source of enrichment. This is the sense of the words spoken by her mentor, Daimó, at the most moving point of the play:

> Resteu, resteu en vostra llar, donzella,
> enc que ara us sembli trista i desolada.
> Serveu la visió gran del pas de l'hèroe
> davant dels vostres ulls: tota la vostra
> vida en serà il.luminada; i, sia
> vostra sort quina sia, sempre, sempre,
> en pau reclosa, o bé pel món enduta,
> en calma, en tempestat, en la vellesa,
> en dolors, en salut, en malaltia,
> sempre tindreu a dintre el cor la dolça
> memòria gran d'aquest moment i hora
> en què heu aimat a un hèroe en puresa,
> i la seva presència fugitiva
> haurà signat per sempre més, des d'ara,
> vostre cor jovenil, bla com la cera,
> amb segell immortal.[28]

This is Maragall's last variation on a theme which had haunted him for years. In his relatively short lifetime, he achieved a quite remarkable authority, both through his unremitting honesty as a journalist and a public figure, and through his correspondence and friendships with Castilian writers like Giner de los Ríos, Unamuno, and Azorín. The best of his poetry has a similar authority, however much one misses the scope and richness of Verdaguer. In his complexities and hesitations, however, one is very aware of the difference in generations: in his relationship with *modernisme*, Maragall succeeds, as no previous Catalan poet had done, in turning the potential weaknesses of his temperament into strengths, and in his Germanic affinities (Goethe,

Nietzsche, and later, Novalis), he anticipates an important strain in more recent Catalan poetry.

Modernisme is clearly centered on Barcelona, and Maragall, despite his very real feeling for landscape, is essentially an urban poet. Valencia and Mallorca, on the other hand, create their own verse traditions in the second half of the nineteenth century, and these continue to reflect the social and linguistic fragmentation which had taken place in the early stages of the Decadence. With few exceptions, nineteenth-century Valencian poetry hardly rises above respectable mediocrity: it is significant, for instance, that the Valencian *Jocs florals*, established in 1879, were bilingual, and were dominated somewhat tyrannically by one of the few genuine poets of the time, Teodor Llorente (1836-1911), who, despite some excellent songs and descriptive poems, too often falls back on the commonplaces of the *Renaixença* tradition.

In Mallorca, the situation is much more promising: here one can speak of a genuine school of poetry, with certain distinctive features lacking in other Catalan poetry of the time. Some of these can already be seen in one of the earliest Mallorcan poets, Josep Lluís Pons i Gallarza (1823-94): a purity of diction and a neo-classical restraint in the handling of patriotic themes, as in his fine poem *L'olivera mallorquina*. The best of the Mallorcan poets, Joan Alcover (1854-1926) and Miquel Costa i Llobera (1854-1922), were exact contemporaries, though Alcover, who began as a poet in Spanish, only turned to Catalan under the stress of personal bereavement. His own explanation of the change—'llavors tota parla que no fos la materna va rebutjar-la el llavi febrosenc, com el contacte de quelcon inexpressiu, fred i metàl.lic'[29]—suggests the urgency, if not the measured dignity, of the elegies contained in his first collection, *Cap al tard* (1909), and his instinctive sense of poetic structure is still more evident in his second book, *Poemes bíblics* (1918), a series of biblical narratives in which the personal note of the earlier poems gives way to an almost Parnassian objectivity.

It is the same kind of clarity, seen in terms of classical, Mediterranean values, which one finds in the poems of Costa i Llobera, a priest whose Romantic feeling for landscape and sense of Christian vocation was controlled by a deep preoccupation with classical forms. His best volume, *Horacianes* (1906), not only shows great skill in the use of classical metres, but also a belief in the objectifying power of art which is very different from the *modernista* criterion of intuition. In Costa, as in other Mallorcan poets, there is a sense of belonging to a Mediterranean world which embraces both the pagan and the Christian traditions. And in Costa particularly, the serenity of the vision is matched by a purity of language which still seems surprisingly modern.

The independence of both Costa and Alcover was clearly recognised by the next generation of Catalan poets. The conscious artistry of their best work, and above all its civilised, 'Mediterranean' quality, came to be seen as a desirable alternative to the undisciplined introspectiveness of *modernisme*. The chief agent in this process was Josep Carner (see below, pp. 99-101), the most active and versatile of the younger poets, for whom the influence of Costa came at a crucial stage in his early career. In the words of Miquel Ferrà:

La influencia de Miquel Costa en Cataluña se hizo sentir principalmente con sus luminosas *Horacianes* ... Quien señaló en esta ocasión a la juventud catalana el valor del magisterio de Costa y Llobera fue José Carner, uno de los que más han cotizado la influencia de Mallorca en el ennoblecimiento del lenguaje y la forma poética.[30]

One sign of the times is the series of lectures by Mallorcan writers organised by the *Ateneu Barcelonès* in 1904. It was on this occasion that both Costa and Alcover made their most important critical statements: Costa's lecture contains an impressive attack on Maragall's theory of 'la paraula viva', in favour of conscious craftsmanship and classical balance; Alcover, for his part, emphasises the artist's need to free himself from the limitations of a particular school, and to communicate with the widest possible audience. Both criteria—lucidity and civic responsibility—were shortly to become guiding principles in a new cultural movement—*noucentisme*—which in turn was to bring its own limitations. For these, neither Costa nor Alcover can be blamed: their views of art are the direct product of their poetic experience, an example of integrity made possible, perhaps, by the very fact of their isolation.

NOTES

1. See R. F. Brown, 'The Romantic novel in Catalonia', *HR*, XIII (1945), 294-323. For Cabanyes and Piferrer, see E. Allison Peers, *A history of the Romantic Movement in Spain* (Cambridge, 1940), 2 vols., I, 312-14 and II, 228-9 respectively.

2. See Josep Robrenyo, *Teatre revolucionari*, ed. J. Ll. Marfany, *AC* (Barcelona, 1965), and also J. M. Poblet, *Les arrels del teatre català* (Barcelona, 1965), 41-71.

3. 'Lemosí' or 'llemosí' = French 'limousin', the name given to one of the areas most closely associated with medieval Provençal poetry, and for a long time wrongly regarded as synonymous with 'Catalan'. *Jocs florals* (literally, 'Floral games') was the title originally given to the literary contests organised in the fourteenth century by the *Sobregaia companhia dels set trobadors* (see above, p. 37), in which the winners were awarded jewels in the form of flowers. The *Jocs* are still celebrated regularly at the present day, though since the Civil War it has not been possible to hold them in Catalonia itself.

4. See Carles Riba, 'Entorn de les trobes d'Aribau', *Obres completes*, II, 433-54.

5. 'But now, torn from their bed by waves and lightning, the sharp rocks and foundations of Calpe [i.e., of Gibraltar, one of the two Pillars of Hercules] emerge into the vast space, filling its void with their sheer blocks and slabs, to see the beautiful light they had never seen before. And terrified by the chaos, they plunge down again on stones which yesterday served them as base, and among the dark caverns of the raging sea they thunder and grind in the great upheaval. The marriage-bed of the Hesperides sinks down, their summits, breaking free from their roots, settle into the valleys, and Atlantis bursts into terrible shrieks, like a woman in childbirth who utters her dying groans'.

6. 'the ageing sun, groping for his fair hair'.

7. 'burning the winter clouds like spiders' webs'.

8. 'When he comes to the ridge of the mountains, he remembers Guifre and his troops. Regretfully he looks back; how beautiful Roussillon seems to his eyes, encircled by a line of beacons, set one by one on every peak. On each hilltop which surrounds the plain of Ruscino, there is a tower, a fair

tower which reaches to the sky, bearing aloft the star which crowns it like a jewel'.

9. 'I am at the inn of Providence, served like a king by the queen's own hand. She gives me wine from her own vine; she gives me bread, gives and cuts it for me'.

10. See Carles Riba, 'Pròleg a una antologia de Jacint Verdaguer', op. cit., 272.

11. Vilanova is the first real humorist of the *Renaixença*. His sketches of city life are finely observed, and contain passages of excellent dialogue. For the most part, however, they are lacking in depth, and one misses the sense of form which is the mark of the genuine short story writer. See Antoni Vilanova's preface to the *Obres completes* (Barcelona, 1949).

12. On Yxart, see the interesting essay by Joan Triadú, 'Josep Yxart en el seu temps', included in *La literatura catalana i el poble* (Barcelona, 1961), 34-47. Oller's friendship with Yxart and Joan Sardà (1851-98), the two outstanding professional critics of the time, had a lasting effect on his own work, and the loss which he felt at their early deaths certainly contributed to the decline in his literary production after 1900.

13. 'The dawn of the twentieth century found me in a terrible state of moral depression ... feeling myself in complete opposition to the themes and tendencies which were taking shape in the new art then called *modernisme*, I was filled with discouragement and at the same time with a great revulsion towards the idea of continuing to write'.

14. 'the great amount of poetry which the natural at times contains for anyone capable of observing it'.

15. 'Order, rules, ordinary habit, financial profit, will always stifle feeling'.

16. 'And standing on a tree-trunk, I looked over the wall. Oh God, what joy! ... on the other side there were streets and people; below me, two children fair as gold were playing; what happiness in their laughter and jumping! But then a woman came out of a door: children, your father's coming, she said, as a man already lifted them in his arms ... wild, as all men are, and I heard his words and loving kisses ... and I wept as he did; for he was weeping! That all passed; childish things! Later, grown-up, I have wished for the joy of Earth only in the cloister. But today I ask myself: what have you done, woman, for your God and Master? ...'

17. Josep Soler i Miquel, a close friend of Maragall, committed suicide in 1897, at the age of 36. His short essay, 'Decadentismo', included in his posthumous *Escritos* (1898), concludes: 'De la vulgaridad naturalista, de la verbosidad convencional y hueca, formada y fría, ya reniega el alma, que desea la invención *imaginaria* viviente, la palabra que enuncia sincera'.

18. *Modernisme* produced one great architect, Antoni Gaudí (1852-1926). It should also be remembered that Picasso spent several years in Barcelona in the late 1890s, and was influenced by some of the painters of the time, notably Isidre Nonell (1873-1911).

19. As organiser of the *Festes modernistes de Sitges* and as the dominating personality in the group of *Els quatre gats*, the famous *modernista* café, Rusiñol provided the essential focal points of the whole movement. Much of his own literary work is characterised by pessimism and *fin-de-siècle* melancholy. He also had a justified reputation as a humorist, and several of his comedies, like *Els savis de Vilatrista* (1907; written in collaboration with Gregorio Martínez Sierra) and the stage version of *L'auca del Senyor*

Esteve (1917), are still frequently performed. For Rusiñol's work as a novelist, and his somewhat equivocal attitude to *modernisme*, see below, p. 107.

20. 'La obra de Santiago Rusiñol', *Obres completes*, II, 130.

21. 'At each mortal outburst people turn trembling: advancing cruelty, retreating fear divide the world between them ... watching the child which sucks the breast of its sighing mother, the father frowns'.

22. 'Las leyes' (1893), *Obres completes*, II, 399.

23. 'Conflict is repellent to my nature, which seeks in everything a centre of harmony and serenity; but those who take part in it interest me greatly, since they enjoy an aspect of life which I have never experienced'.

24. On the genesis of *El comte Arnau,* see Arthur Terry, *La poesia de Joan Maragall* (Barcelona, 1963), 133-58.

25. 'The power of rhythm brings you words, and only later do you see the thought which these convey: this is revelation through form'.

26. 'I cannot conceive the next life as separate from this one ... To make human life, both earthly and supernatural, into a single whole, that is my own most personal interpretation of the poem, which is nothing less than the basic preoccupation of my life'.

27. The immediate cause of the rising was the call-up of the Catalan reserves to fight in the war in Morocco. The protest which followed led to five days of rioting which was brutally suppressed by the Home Secretary of the time, La Cierva. Among those executed afterwards was Francisco Ferrer, a theoretical anarchist who had taken no part in the rising, and on whose behalf Maragall tried unsuccessfully to intervene. For a good short summary of events and their consequences, see Gerald Brenan, *The Spanish labyrinth* (Cambridge, 1943), 34-5.
On the complex relationship between Maragall's writings of this time, which include the poem *Oda nova a Barcelona* and the essays *Ah! Barcelona ...*, *La iglésia cremada,* and *La ciutat del perdó,* see Josep Benet, *Maragall i la Setmana Tràgica* (Barcelona, 1963), and also Arthur Terry, 'The *Cant espiritual* of Joan Maragall', *BHS,* XXXVIII (1961), 265-73.

28. 'Stay, stay here, girl, where you were born, though now the place may seem sad and desolate. Serve the great vision of the hero who passed before your eyes: it will illuminate your whole life; and whatever your fate may be, always, always, withdrawn in peace or driven through the world, in calm, in tempest, in old age, in grief, in health or sickness, always you will have within your heart the great, dear memory of the hour and moment when you loved a hero in absolute purity, and his fleeting presence will have stamped for ever more, from this time on, your young heart, soft as wax, with an immortal seal'.

29. 'then my feverish lips rejected every form of speech but their own, like the contact of something inexpressive, cold and metallic'.

30. Quoted by Albert Manent in his excellent book *Josep Carner i el noucentisme* (Barcelona, 1969), 71.

Chapter 4

THE TWENTIETH CENTURY

I. POETRY: NOUCENTISME AND AVANT-GARDE

THE YEAR 1906 IS NORMALLY regarded as a watershed in the history of modern Catalan literature. Before this, even the most original writers are related in one way or another to the *Renaixença*, even though some of them, like Maragall, are directly concerned with the political and social events of the time. It is, in fact, a new sense of the relations between politics and culture which determines the next phase of literary activity —one which lasts, with certain deviations, until the Civil War. What crystallises the Catalan political movements of the period is the colonial disaster of 1898: the effects of this on the Catalan economy and the growing sense of alienation from the central government were among the chief motives behind the foundation of the *Lliga regionalista* (1901) and the popular front movement, *Solidaritat catalana* (1906). Under the leadership of Enric Prat de la Riba (1870-1917), eventually to become the first President of the *Mancomunitat* (1913), cultural life comes to be regarded for the first time as an essential component in the political future of Catalonia.[1] Thus 1906 is not only the year of Prat's own manifesto, *La nacionalitat catalana*, but also of the first International Congress of the Catalan Language (followed in 1907 by the foundation of the *Institut d'Estudis Catalans*), and of the first important writings of Eugeni d'Ors (1882-1954) and Josep Carner (1884-1970), the leading figures in the movement which came to be known as *noucentisme*.[2]

The aims of the *noucentistes* were made insistently clear in

97

the *Glosari* which Ors published over a period of twelve years under the name of 'Xènius'. One of Ors's key phrases is 'art arbitrari': the idea that art should be 'arbitrary' in the sense of breaking completely with the existing tradition, with what he calls the 'rusticity' of nineteenth-century Catalan literature. Behind this lies the possibility of reinstating an alternative tradition, the one which has been broken off at the Renaissance. At this point, the qualifications begin: if Martorell and Roiç de Corella are the last classical writers in Catalan, there can be no question of carrying on from them in a literal sense; what is needed is a new type of humanism which will fulfil a similar function in modern terms, and a sense of the language as it might have developed normally after the fifteenth century. In the widest terms, both society and the arts are to share the same concept of urbanity (another key word of the time), and this will be possible precisely because it is to be the guiding principle of official patronage.[3]

What *noucentisme* meant in poetic terms can be seen from Ors's preface to *La muntanya d'ametistes* (1908), the first book of poems by Guerau de Liost, the pen-name of Jaume Bofill i Mates (1878-1933). The mountain of the title is a real one—the Montseny—whose various aspects are described in a mass of closely observed detail. At the same time, the effect is very different from the impressionistically rendered landscapes of the *modernistes*: the sacramental overtones of the description ('les alzines que cremen en el fumós altar'[4] is a typical image) are purely aesthetic in their intention, and the clinical precision of the language and the strict verse forms strengthen the sense of a nature which has been disciplined and reshaped in the interests of art. For Ors, this is the real triumph of these poems: the poet, he explains, has 'imprisoned Nature' and judged it by the canons of the City, that is to say, in terms of intellectual rigour and delight in craftsmanship. In one of his later collections, *La ciutat d'ivori* (1918), Guerau de Liost offers his own version of the Ideal City, which reflects very accurately the *noucentista* concern with civility:

...Bella ciutat de marbre del món exterior,
esdevinguda aurífica dins un esguard d'amor!

Ets tota laborada amb ordenat esment.
Et purifica el viure magnànim i cruent.

I, per damunt la frèvola grandesa terrenal,
empunyaràs la palma del seny—que és immortal.[5]

The sense of collective responsibility which runs through these poems hardly prepares one for the inventiveness and irony of his other collections, notably *Somnis* (1913) and *Sàtires* (1928). In the first of these, the medievalism which seems to have come naturally to Guerau de Liost is an important part of the fantasies in which he imagines a series of situations (among them, his own birth and death and a journey to Hell) of which he has no conscious experience. The humour and the rich social and domestic detail of these poems look forward to the more pointed irony of his last collection, *Sàtires*. By this stage, the vision of the ideal state has succumbed to the realities of the Primo de Rivera dictatorship, and many of these superbly accomplished poems are directed against those members of his own class who have compromised with the times. And to the last, Guerau de Liost retains a moral independence which, though in one sense it is a perfect expression of *noucentisme*, seems so basic to his whole temperament that it hardly needs a literary programme to support it.

The other poet associated with the beginnings of *noucentisme* is Josep Carner, a close friend of Guerau de Liost, whose collected poems span almost seventy years of literary activity. Like *La muntanya d'ametistes*, Carner's second volume, *Els fruits saborosos* (1906), was an important index to the new sensibility: what the two books have in common is a sense of stylisation, of style as something which imposes an aesthetic distance on the subject matter. Carner's own stratagem consists in taking a number of common situations from middle-class life and treating them in the manner of the classical eclogue. The effect is curiously ambivalent: the classical overtones (which extend to the names of the characters) are sentimentalised, and the middle-class world is seen through a haze of pastoral melancholy. Seen in the context of the time, these poems are Carner's contribution to the vision of the Ideal City; in them, literary style is used to indicate a style of living based on intelligence, good sense, and elegance. These qualities, in fact, sum up a great deal of Carner's later and more mature poetry. Compared with Guerau de Liost, he is more fluent, less severe, and ultimately, perhaps, less serious. In view of his enormous range and technical skill, this may seem an unfair criticism. Though the elegance of his earlier poems seems at times over-fastidious, it would be wrong to think of him as an orthodox exponent of *noucentisme*: what appealed to him in the aims of the movement, one feels, was the emphasis on clarity of structure and the possibilities it gave for anti-Romantic irony, and much less its conscious attempt to reinstate an interrupted tradition.

The civilised humour of Carner's early poems, much less sharp than that of Guerau de Liost, gave them a balance and an assurance which set the tone for the literary atmosphere of the time. In 1921, however, he entered the Consular Service, a decision which was to take him to Geneva, Costa Rica, Mexico, and finally to Brussels, where he spent the last twenty-five years of his life. The effect on his poetry was very marked. Whatever the motives for his voluntary exile,[6] his new poems show a deeper sense of compassion and a tendency to speculate on meta-physical questions which go far beyond the range of his earlier work. Above all, perhaps, he seems to have learnt how to use his talent for acute observation as the basis for a new kind of realism in which the moral comment is carried into the details of the poem. This in itself is a sign of the increasing moral complexity of the later poems. In *Nabi* (1941), one of the three or four best modern Catalan poems of some length, Carner uses the biblical story of Jonah as a means of focusing some of his deepest pre-occupations. Its narrative skill alone would make the poem out-standing: what gives it its real stature, however, is the way in which the alternating voices of faith and doubt are made to coincide, with dramatic inevitability, in the concluding vision of hope:

> Car tota cosa, tret de Déu, és fugissera.
> ¿Qui dirà mai ses menes d'eternes resplendors
> en parla forastera
> i amb llavi farfallós?
> Adéu, però, grans grapes de càstig i avarícia!
> Morir per a la nova naixó, clara delícia!
> Només amor esdevindrà l'home rebel.
> Car ultrapassaràs del Pare la justícia,
> oh maternal condícia
> del brossat, de les pomes i la mel![7]

In this and other poems of his final phase, the nonchalance of Carner's earlier work has resolved itself into an emotional authority which is all the more impressive for its restraint and its sense of collective responsibility in the face of historical circumstances very different from those under which he began to write.

No one faced up more singlemindedly to the cultural implications of *noucentisme* than Carles Riba (1893-1959), an enormously gifted poet and translator,[8] and beyond question the most intelligent literary critic of his generation. Riba's first mature poems were collected in the two books of *Estances* (1913-1919; 1920-30). The first book has been described as a 'brilliant cultural exercise'. On the surface, at least, this seems just: the echoes of Ausias March and the *stilnovisti* seem part of a carefully calculated attempt to restore the interrupted tradition, precisely as Ors had recommended. Yet the real value of the poems goes deeper than this: Riba is not so much concerned with an academic kind of eclecticism as with consciously selecting certain models which will help him to express his own preoccupations. Like most of Riba's later work, these are personal poems, not in a confessional sense, but in their consistent attempt to explore real psychological states by means of certain traditional abstractions: mind, soul, desire, and the senses. In the second book, the medieval influences give way to those of the German Romantics and the French Symbolists, in particular Goethe, Hölderlin, Mallarmé, and Valéry. In these later poems, Riba's mastery of fixed forms is thrown into relief by the extraordinary flexibility of the syntax; and though, in a sense, he is always a reticent poet, these are poems which explore very movingly the vulnerability of human love. Riba's next collection, *Tres suites* (1930-35), is both denser and more restricted in content, a deliberate approach to the notion of *poésie pure* which, for all its apparent hermeticism, probably marked a decisive point in his poetic development.[9] By comparison, his other poems of the thirties, eventually collected in *Del joc i del foc* (1946), seem hesitant and uncertain in their intention, and there are moments when Riba seems dissatisfied with his own skill.

Any such doubts were interrupted by the Civil War and the period of exile which followed it. The *Elegies de Bierville* (1943) reflect the experience of these years on a scale which one could hardly have imagined from Riba's earlier verse. As poems about exile, they present an account of personal suffering reduced to its basic elements so that it can stand for the collective experience. At the same time, the fact that the later poems in the sequence were written after Riba's decision to return to Catalonia gives them a double movement—exile and return—which appears in various forms: spiritual privation and restoration, the death and rebirth of the soul, a sense of being temporarily withdrawn from the collective life in order to participate in it with greater knowledge:

...era girat a mi que escoltava crèixer l'anunci
   de no sé quina mar interior, madurant
  lluny dins meu en illes d'encara impotent melodia;
    canvi o naixença—era igual: era una mar i el seu vent.[10]

This spiritual exploration is seen in terms both of personal experience and of certain basic mythical patterns (the Orphic adept's descent into Hades, Ulysses's return to Ithaca) which gradually lead to a recognition of the Christian God. This is a new note in Riba's poetry, and in his last two collections, *Salvatge cor* (1952) and *Esbós de tres oratoris* (1957), the patient speculations of the *Elegies* give way to a more dramatic questioning of the possibilities of religious belief.[11] In this final phase, the conscious acknowledgement of doubt and paradox ends in the affirmation of one of Riba's basic insights: that life, in any real sense, implies generosity and the acceptance of 'risk' (one of his key words) as the only means to salvation. In the poems, none of these solutions is completely permanent, and to the end Riba's work shows a coherence and an openness to experience which place him among the major poets of the Symbolist tradition.

Hardly surprisingly, a great deal of the best Catalan poetry of the last fifty years reflects the influence of Carner and Riba. One might argue, in fact, that the surest sign of the vitality of Catalan poetry between the wars is the presence, not only of two or three major poets, but also of a dozen or so interesting minor ones, like J. M. Lòpez-Picó (1886-1959), Marià Manent (1898-   ), and Tomàs Garcés (1901-   ), all of whom tend to share a similar view of poetry, in which purity of language and precision of imagery are related in varying degrees to the dominant modes of Symbolism.

Not every poet of the period falls into this pattern: the deceptively simple lyrics of Clementina Arderiu (1893-   ), the wife of Carles Riba, seem to come directly from her own spontaneous sense of life, without the mediation of literary models. Similarly, though in other respects they are utterly different, the early poems of J. M. Sagarra (1894-1961) suggest a more traditional and egocentric writer who seems completely untouched by the ideals of *noucentisme*. And at the other extreme, there is the impact of certain avant-garde movements—Cubism, Futurism, and Dada—which roughly coincides with the period of political unrest between the death of Prat de la Riba, the outstanding Catalan politician of the early part of the century (1917), and the establishment of the Primo de Rivera dictatorship in 1923.

The crucial figure here is Joan Salvat-Papasseit (1894-1924), an uneven but very original poet about whom critics still tend to disagree. Salvat is the only important working-class poet of the period, though he scarcely fits the usual picture of a proletarian writer. His own statements about poetry tend to be confused and anarchistic, though in practice there is very little social protest in his poems. His reputation for subversiveness comes partly from his statements and partly from his early experimental poetry, which makes use of typographical devices in the manner of Apollinaire and Marinetti. These poems now seem the most derivative part of his work: what rebelliousness they contain is generalised and Romantic, and Salvat talks continually of the liberty and dignity of man, without any real awareness of the class struggle. The best of his later poetry, in fact, comes from a clear acceptance of his own social situation: his sense of the texture of everyday life gives his poems a realism which one hardly finds in the middle-class poets of the time, and the naturalness of the love-poems in *La rosa als llavis* (1923)— the most genuine erotic poetry in modern Catalan—presupposes a kind of security which has nothing at all to do with contemporary literary models.

Salvat-Papasseit died in 1924, when he was only thirty. On the surface, it might seem that *noucentisme* and the avant-garde tradition were incompatible, yet there is one poet, J. V. Foix (1894-   ), whose work bridges the gap with extraordinary skill. Foix's earliest statements on poetry are very similar to those of Carles Riba: both appear to accept the basic aims of *noucentisme*, and particularly the need to restore the broken tradition of Catalan humanism. What is striking in Foix is that he interprets this general preoccupation both more literally and more widely than any of his contemporaries. One of his best-known lines reads: 'M'exalta el nou i m'enamora el vell'.[12] As far as older Catalan poetry is concerned, Foix, significantly, is the only poet of his generation who is prepared to go back as far as Llull. However, it is in his conception of the 'new' that he diverges most sharply from a poet like Riba who, after his early poems, moves steadily in the direction of the Symbolism which Foix rejects. The spectrum of Foix's poetry is much wider than this: at one end of the scale he goes back through Ausias March to the poems of the troubadours, and at the other he is closer to Apollinaire and the Futurists than to Mallarmé.

Something like a third of Foix's published work consists of four collections of prose poems grouped under the general title of *Diari 1918*. The fact that he has chosen to refer this part of his work to a particular year, though many of the individual pieces must have been written later, confirms one's impression that the later work, both poems and prose poems, represents a steady unfolding of the possibilities implied in his very earliest writing. Foix has been loosely described as a surrealist, though this conflicts with his own view of reality. More than once, he has referred to himself as 'un investigador en poesia', not in any clinical or frivolous sense, but simply as an indication that he sees poetry as what he calls an 'objective reality', a reality which is always there, detached from the poet, but always ready to be explored. So he speaks of his prose poems as 'similitudes' (*semblances*), as deliberately oblique attempts to 'realise his personality', and, characteristically, his use of the word 'semblança' is taken directly from a sentence of Llull: 'De les semblances reals davallen les fantàstiques, enaixí com accidents que ixen de substància'.[13] In the fantastic narratives of many of his poems, details which in isolation seem merely surrealistic fall into place as parts of a personal myth which, because it is detached from any autobiographical intentions, can move easily between individual and collective experience. However much his poems approach the condition of waking dreams, Foix insists that the poet is a kind of magician who retains the power to manipulate the elements of his vision. In his later volumes of poetry, particularly *Les irreals omegues* (1948) and *On he deixat les claus...* (1953), the emotional authority with which he is able to write of the Civil War depends precisely on this ability to control the anecdotal elements of a situation in order to raise it to the status of myth. The relative lack of development, which in a different kind of writer might be a weakness, seems natural enough in a poet who sees his task as the exploration of a single truth, which is both unique and indivisible. As a result, Foix has remained extraordinarily faithful to the themes and technique of his early work, while at the same time he has experimented constantly with new material in a way which makes him both the least literary and the most frequently exciting poet of his generation.[14]

II. DRAMA AND FICTION BEFORE 1936

Perhaps the greatest limitation of *noucentisme* was that it encouraged poetry at the expense of other kinds of writing. Such an effect was partly deliberate, and partly the natural consequence of a movement which placed so much emphasis on the need to purify the language itself. This helps to explain the relative poverty of the Catalan theatre before the Civil War: the types of audience which supported the plays of Rusiñol (see above, p. 87) or the working-class drama of Ignasi Iglèsies (1871-1928) remained untouched by the most important literary movement of the time. In the 1920s and '30s, the commercial theatre went its own way; the one really talented dramatist of these years, J. M. Sagarra (see above, p. 103), achieved his success through a series of Romantic plays, sometimes of considerable lyrical power, which were completely divorced from any kind of social reality. This is not to say that serious writers were not aware of the need for a more responsible type of theatre; in terms of practical results, however, there is little to show beyond the first plays of Joan Oliver (1899-   ), a writer whose full importance does not emerge until after 1936.

The situation in fiction is more complex. In 1925, Carles Riba delivered a famous lecture, *Una generació sense novel.la*, in which he argued that the absence of mature novelists was due, not so much to lack of talent, as to the moral poverty of contemporary Catalan society.[15] Significantly, he did not mention Narcís Oller;

what he was hoping for, clearly, was a type of society which would measure up to the ideals of *noucentisme*: 'cal, doncs, un llarg temps, perquè una atmosfera d'humanisme impregni el cos social'.[16]

Looking back to the beginning of the century, one sees yet again the inhibiting effect of *noucentisme*. As we have seen, Oller's last novel, *Pilar Prim* (1906), departs to some extent from the realism of his earlier work. A few years before, the deaths of Yxart and Sardà had put an end to the period of rational, positivist criticism which had sanctioned his previous novels, leaving the way open to the intuitive subjectivism of the *modernistes*. In its way, the originality of *Pilar Prim* is an index to the change in literary mood: it seems no coincidence that its hero, Deberga, is a reader of Nietzsche, and much of the descriptive writing is 'poetic' in a *modernista* sense. These are perhaps minor aspects of a novel which still owes its success to the study of individual psychology and environment, yet they suggest Oller's growing doubts as to the validity of the realistic novel and his difficulties in finding an alternative solution.

The fragmentary nature of *modernista* prose—echoed in poetry by Maragall's theory of 'la paraula viva'—was basically at odds with the idea of an organically constructed novel. One effect of this is a revival of the *quadre de costums*, a type of writing which easily lent itself to the *fin-de-siècle* sensibility, whether as prose poem or short story. The novels of Santiago Rusiñol, for example, are invariably composed of a number of these smaller units. As Maragall pointed out (see above, p. 87), Rusiñol's work is often morbid and devitalised, though there are times when the characteristic *modernista* attitudes are swept aside by bursts of iconoclastic humour. Despite his status as artistic leader, Rusiñol's relations with *modernisme* are a little ambiguous, and his irreverence often appears to be turned against art itself. Only once does he succeed in turning his weaknesses into strengths. This is in *L'auca del Senyor Esteve* (1907), a minor comic masterpiece which, in its way, is a serious, though unrepeatable, solution to the problems of the *modernista* novel. The *auca* of the title is the

Catalan equivalent of the *aleluya* or popular broadsheet tale, told in cartoon-frames, each of which is accompanied by a humorous couplet. The couplets, in Rusiñol's novel, form the chapter headings, and the tale itself describes the rise to prosperity of a family of Barcelona haberdashers. As in other novels of the period, the technique is episodic and fragmentary: yet the deliberate echo of a popular art form creates a distancing effect which allows the author to move easily between satire and nostalgia. And woven into the basic plot is a theme which relates the whole book to one of the central preoccupations of *modernisme*, the position of the artist in a society which one side of his nature rejects. Ramonet, the son of Esteve, attempts to escape from his family by becoming a *modernista*: at the end of the novel, he is about to embark on a career as a sculptor, yet, ironically, he can only do this with the aid of his uncomprehending father: 'En faré perquè *ell* paga el marbre' ('I shall make sculptures because *he's* paying for the marble'). Thus Ramonet's liberation through art is strictly relative, and the final paradox is both an assertion and a criticism of *modernista* values.

After *L'auca del Senyor Esteve*, Rusiñol's fiction suffers increasingly from the contradictions which he himself had diagnosed in his most successful work. In other novelists of the beginning of the century, a different kind of tension can be seen, which will eventually help to bring about the collapse of the *modernista* novel as a whole. In general terms, the problem of such writers is to find a means of reconciling the basic principles of realism with the demands of the new subjectivity. One result of this is an insistence on the more 'decadent' aspects of Romanticism. The erotic mysticism one finds in the early novels of Prudenci Bertrana (1861-1942)—*Josafat* (1906) and *Els nàufrags* (1907)—is only one attempt to break through the limitations of conventional narrative into a more subjective and 'poetic' world. In other novelists, this accounts for the powerful fantasy element contained in what, on the surface, often appears to be naturalistic writing, and it is precisely in this area that the most impressive achievements of the *modernista* novel are to be found.

The dominant mode of fiction between 1900 and 1907 is the rural novel, whose chief exponents are Ramon Casellas (1855-1910), Marià Vayreda (1850-1903), Josep Pous i Pagès (1873-(1952), and Víctor Català (the pen-name of Caterina Albert; 1869-1966). The best-known work of this group is Víctor Català's novel *Solitud* (1905), a story of great power and psychological penetration, which seems deliberately to play off the *modernista* attitude to nature against the determinism of the Naturalists.[17] Its most distinguished predecessor is Ramon Casellas's *Els sots feréstecs* (1901), with which it has a good deal in common. Both Casellas and Víctor Català are exploiting a tendency which is already established in the earlier, more conventional fiction of the *costumista* variety. But where earlier *costumisme* had tended to be idyllic and sentimental, the new version of ruralism is altogether grimmer. The nearest parallel here is with the rural dramas of Guimerà: in fiction, however, such a vision of nature involves a partial reassessment of narrative form, and it is here that one sees most clearly how the deliberately fragmented structure encouraged by *modernisme* leads in the direction of fantasy and Symbolism. Both novelists, in fact, are engaged in the same task: the transformation of the older type of realism through an awareness of *modernista* aesthetics. Neither of their novels can be adequately judged in realistic terms. In *Els sots feréstecs*, the effect is that of an extended metaphor: the story of a single obsession in which the neurotic terrors of the protagonist—a country priest whose fear of being 'buried alive' in the mountains hovers frighteningly on the borders of reality—are presented in purely artistic terms. *Solitud*, by comparison, is less insulated from real life, and its symbolism is richer, if less coherent. The emergence of the central character, Mila, from adolescence into womanhood involves two conflicting views of nature. One is the Rousseauesque vision of the earlier Romantics, symbolised by the figure of the shepherd, Gaietà; the other feeds on a sense of violence and evil, and it is this which prevails. In such a setting, Mila's development becomes an initiation into the darker reaches of the imagination, a recognition of the disturbing and powerful

forces which lie beneath the *modernista* faith in intuition.
Ultimately, both novels are highly personal solutions to a problem
which underlies the *modernista* novel as a whole. It is difficult to
see how the rural novel, conceived in these terms, could have
developed further: as it was, Casellas wrote no more novels, and,
significantly, all Víctor Català's important books—*Solitud* and
the three collections of stories, *Drames rurals* (1902), *Ombrívoles*
(1904), and *Caires vius* (1907)—were published within a space of
six years.

Several other novelists of the time do, in fact, continue to work
in this manner, though more often than not in the form of the
short story. The one notable exception to this is Pous i Pagès, the
author of *La vida i la mort d'En Jordi Fraginals* (1912), a novel
which seems quite deliberately to mark the passing of *modernisme*.
Curiously enough, the first four parts of the novel read like a
serious and well-executed attempt to reinstate the more conventional and objective type of rural novel. The last part, however, is
different: the final illness and suicide of the chief character imply
the total collapse of the reality which has been so carefully built
up in the earlier stages of the book. One suspects that Unamuno's
praise of *Jordi Fraginals*—'la novela es novela, toda una novela y
no más que una novela' [18]—was directed particularly at these
closing chapters: the 'tragic sense of life' which they convey
comes not only from the final dissolution of a strong-willed protagonist, but also from the sense in which the author himself
appears to accept the final impasse of the *modernista* sensibility. [19]

As a genre, then, the rural novel hardly survived the first impact of *noucentisme*. One of the basic attitudes of the new movement was its anti-ruralism, its desire to impose order on what it
regarded, justly or otherwise, as a source of Romantic imprecision.
Combined with this, however, was an attack on the novel as a
whole, on the grounds of its irrelevance to the creation of the
Ideal City whose achievement still lay in the future. The phrase
of Carles Riba's already quoted—'cal, doncs, un llarg temps,
perquè una atmosfera d'humanisme envolti i impregni el cos
social' [20]—merely echoes an argument which had first appeared

nearly twenty years before. To ignore the achievement of Oller and the *modernistes* now seems perverse, though at the time the confrontation with *modernisme* was a necessary condition of success in other directions. As we have seen, the *modernista* novel itself suffered from the more general crisis of Naturalism; at least by 1912, the novel as a genre was discredited as part of the new orthodoxy, and there are few signs of a serious revival before the mid-1920s. There are occasions, even, when the sense of disorientation which Riba describes in his lecture seems to be confirmed by the novelists themselves: in an interview given in 1926, Víctor Català refers to the Catalan novel as a 'nineteenth-century genre'; two years later, Joan Puig i Ferrater (1882-1956), in his confessional novel *Vida interior d'un escriptor*, reveals his sense of frustration at the intellectual superiority of the *noucentistes*.

This feeling of alienation is partly a matter of language, of the inability to achieve the degree of linguistic refinement demanded by the most influential critics of the time.[21] For the majority of the *noucentistes*, on the other hand, prose is something to be cultivated separately from the novel, either in the form of the short story or of translations of foreign classics. The few attempts at a more extended type of fiction are novels in name only: the most celebrated, Eugeni d'Ors's *La ben plantada* (1912), is, as Unamuno said, 'un pequeño evangelio estético político', a rhetorical meditation on an ideal woman who symbolises the coming of the new classicism.

The one prose-writer of an older generation to be accepted by the *noucentistes* was Joaquim Ruyra (1858-1939). The reasons for this are partly literary, partly linguistic. Ruyra's first volume of stories, *Marines i boscatges* (1904), later included in *Pinya de rosa* (1920), already shows a concern for style and precision of language which sets it apart from the contemporary rural novel. This is all the more striking since Ruyra's own subjects are invariably rural: his descriptions of the landscape and inhabitants of the Costa Brava and its interior have an authority which comes partly from the accurate registering of local idiom and partly from sympathetic observation. It is this last feature above all which gives his stories their peculiar distinctiveness: where the rural novel is often violent and pessimistic, Ruyra's whole vision is based on a religious sense of goodness and simplicity. The compactness of his stories (his one attempt at a full-length novel was never completed[22]) is partly a question of tone: even in those which are not told in the first person, one is aware of the narrator's voice which controls the succession of events. The characteristic temper of this voice is gently ironical, and Catalan critics have often spoken of Ruyra's 'Franciscanism'—a term which several of his best stories, notably *Les coses benignes* (1925), seem deliberately to invite. Yet his concern for language is not merely a part of his sympathy for people and natural objects. As the preface to *Pinya de rosa* makes clear, Ruyra was very conscious of the linguistic aims of *noucentisme*, and it is this, as much as anything, which explains the extraordinary modernity of his prose.[23]

Though by 1925 the novel had begun to revive, it was precisely this sense of artistry which was lacking in the more substantial novelists of the period—writers like Puig i Ferrater and Prudenci Bertrana, whose books all too often give the impression of thinly fictionalised autobiography. In the late 1920s and early '30s, however, there are signs of a more serious approach to fiction in the early novels and stories of Miquel Llor (1894-1966), Llorenç Villalonga (1897-   ), Joan Oliver (1899-   ), Xavier Berenguel (1905-   ), and Salvador Espriu (1914-   ). The work of all these writers is fairly modest in scale, but in each of them one is aware of a poise and a sense of the complexity of human relationships which had been lost to Catalan fiction since Narcís Oller. In Villalonga in particular, poise takes the form of a consciously aristocratic snobbery through which the semi-feudal society of Mallorca is filtered with affectionate irony, a note which he has sustained with great brilliance through a whole series of books, from *Mort de dama* (1931) to *Bearn* (1961), one of the most outstanding novels published since the Civil War.

In some of the best writers of the 1930s there is an obvious widening of scope. One example of this is the trilogy *Novel.les de l'Ebre* (*Terres de l'Ebre* (1932); *Camins de nit* (1935); *Tino Costa* (1947)) by Sebastià Juan Arbó (1902-   ), which demonstrates very forcefully the continuing relevance of the rural novel as a means of presenting unfamiliar areas of life. But the most striking reminder of the geographical and social variety of Catalonia is the work of Josep Pla (1897-   ), an extremely prolific writer who, though to some extent he shares the *noucentista* prejudice against the novel, is beyond any doubt the most gifted social observer of the last fifty years. Though he has written biographies and a certain amount of fiction, Pla's favourite form is the personal travel diary. The title of one of his earliest books, *Coses vistes* (1925), could stand for most of his work: his endless curiosity and apparently spontaneous capacity for verbalising his experience are conveyed in a style whose sheer readability conceals a great deal of literary skill. In many ways, Pla is the most professional of living Catalan authors: though a strong, and at times pessimistic, personality comes through his books, one's main impression is of normality—the normality of a writer who has confidently accepted a particular literary situation and whose work itself, in its unfailing regularity, has helped to keep alive a whole tradition of writing and communication through the difficult circumstances of the 1940s and '50s.

III. THE CIVIL WAR TO THE PRESENT DAY

The Civil War of 1936-39 brought about the complete collapse of Catalan political institutions and to a great extent of the cultural tradition which had been patiently built up over the previous forty years. The war itself produced a few fine poems, notably by two gifted poets who died young, Bartolomeu Rosselló-Pòrcel (1913-18) and Màrius Torres (1910-42). After the Republican defeat, many writers went into exile, in some cases permanently. For those who remained or returned in the early 1940s, the literary situation could hardly have been more discouraging: the banning of Catalan in schools, the severe restrictions on publication, and the general vindictiveness of the central government towards any manifestations of Catalan culture made this a period of ephemeral little magazines and other clandestine publications. By the mid-1950s this situation had eased a little,[24] and one could begin to observe two distinct types of reaction on the part of Catalan writers. On the one hand, there was a high-minded though anachronistic attempt to write as if circumstances were still normal, and on the other, there were the beginnings of a more socially conscious kind of writing, represented by the two most influential poets of the post-war period, Salvador Espriu and Pere Quart. In this situation, the death of Carles Riba in 1959 seemed like the end of an epoch: though the *Elegies de Bierville* had been the finest poems to come out of the Civil War, the Symbolist tradition seemed to have come to an end with its most distinguished practitioner.

Neither Espriu nor Pere Quart was exactly a new writer. Pere Quart is the pseudonym of Joan Oliver (see above, p. 106), a writer who had published fiction and verse in the 1930s and had begun to make a name as a dramatist during the Civil War with plays like *Allò que tal vegada s'esdevingué* (1936) and *La fam* (1938). Basically, Pere Quart is a serious moralist who is also a superb entertainer: a middle-class writer whose dislike of bourgeois complacency has made him the most accomplished satirist of his generation. His poetry, particularly in his last two collections, *Vacances pagades* (1961) and *Circumstàncies* (1968), breaks every rule of 'fine writing': it is colloquial, often to the point of coarseness, realistic, totally unrhetorical, and full of self-mockery. As he says in one of his prefaces:

> Pere Quart, pel que sembla prefereix avui—i també en poesia, el desordre creador i la dolorosa inquietud esperançada,[25]

words which suggest very well the directness, and also the occasional poignancy, of his best verse.

Espriu is the more complex of the two writers, and the finer poet. Like Joan Oliver, he has worked in more than one genre. The maturity of his first two books of poems, *Cementiri de Sinera*

(1946) and *Les cançons d'Ariadna* (1949), probably reflects his earlier experience as a prose-writer. Several of the older stories written in the 1930s already show what was to become a basic polarity in his work: a controlled anger at the false values of the urban middle classes (an attitude he shares with Oliver) and an elegiac tenderness towards the vanishing rural and mercantile community of Arenys de Mar, the 'Sinera' of his poems and fiction. Since the Civil War, Espriu has published only three stories, of which *Tres sorores* is a small masterpiece, the nearest thing in Catalan to Joyce's 'The Dead'. The full complexity of his reactions to the war appeared for the first time in his 'improvisation for puppets', *Primera història d'Esther* (1948). Here, by imagining the performance of a play on the biblical episode of Esther in the small Catalan town of Sinera, Espriu is able to superimpose the Old Testament story on the world of his own childhood. Like all his best work, this depends for part of its effect on the extraordinary linguistic agility with which he creates a situation in which the barriers of time and place are abolished, and where the dead generations of Sinera are as real to the biblical characters as they are to the author himself. And in the final speech of the showman to the audience, the contemporary reference becomes even clearer:

> Eviteu el màxim crim, el pecat de la guerra entre germans. Penseu que el mirall de la veritat s'esmicolà a l'origen en fragments petitíssims, i cada un dels trossos recull tanmateix una engruna d'autèntica llum.[26]

In his poems, Espriu has meditated constantly, through both elegy and satire, on the need to come to terms with death, without losing faith in the value of life. Since the war, he has extended the range of his writing in the direction of public issues. This is particularly clear in his best-known collection, *La pell de brau* (1960), a sequence in which the collective situation of the Peninsular peoples is focused through themes and images taken from the history of the Jews in exile. There is no doubt that this book did more than anything else to establish Espriu as the spokesman of the post-war generation, sometimes at the expense of his other writing. But it is equally obvious that his view of the collective situation is also an intensely personal one, and that failure to realise this can only over-simplify an achievement of great integrity and emotional complexity.

In the early 1960s, the poetry of Espriu and Pere Quart was often used to justify the arguments for 'social realism' which ran through the critical statements of the time. In so far as they amounted to a literary programme, these arguments tended to be over-rigid and more limiting than the post-Symbolist tradition they often attacked. Looking back over the new poetry of the last ten years, however, one can see that the demand for greater contemporary awareness was worth making. What is most valuable in the 'realist' attitude is the stress which it places on personal experience, and this is exactly what one finds, for example, in the best of the new poets, Gabriel Ferrater (1922-1972). Ferrater's three volumes of poems, now collected in *Les dones i els dies* (1968), are fluent and intelligent, and it is precisely the strength of his private convictions and the sense of the individual's struggle to achieve some kind of happiness which set him apart from lesser poets who have tried too consciously to assume a public voice. At the same time, it is hardly enough to call Ferrater a 'poet of experience': what really distinguishes him is his persistent attempt to show how experience itself is constantly reshaped in the mind, and how this process adds up to the sense of an individual life. It is clear, also, that his moral attitudes do not depend on any large-scale system of beliefs. Like Thomas Hardy, a poet he particularly admired, Ferrater wrote simply from a sense of his own life, from a sense that the suddenly surfacing perceptions of life can fit whole and without compromise into poems. Or, as he put it in the preface to his first collection, *Da nuces pueris* (1960):

Entenc la poesia com la descripció, passant de moment a moment, de la vida moral d'un home ordinari, com ho sóc jo ...Quan escric una poesia, l'única cosa que m'ocupa i em costa és de definir ben bé la meva actitud moral, o sigui la distància que hi ha entre el sentiment que la poesia exposa i el que en podríem dir el centre de la meva imaginació.[27]

One of the most striking features of the post-war literary scene is the number of writers who have produced work in more than one genre, and particularly the number of novelists who have also written plays. Several older writers have published some of their best work since 1950; Llorenç Villalonga (see above, p. 112) is one example; another is Mercè Rodoreda (1909-   ), whose novel *La Plaça del Diamant* (1962), the story of a working-class woman in the Barcelona of the 1930s and '40s, is perhaps the finest work of fiction to have appeared since the Civil War. The book has been justly praised, both for its rendering of the details of ordinary life and for its moments of poetic intensity. Yet the latter are in no sense pieces of 'fine writing': the first-person narrative remains firmly rooted in the consciousness of the central character, whose own experience is allowed to create the simple, but moving, symbols which give shape to her story.

Among the more serious novelists now writing, at least two dozen names stand out, and the shortest list would have to include Joan Sales (1912-   ), Manuel Pedrolo (1918-   ), Maria Aurèlia Capmany (1918-   ), Jordi Sarsanedas (1924-   ), Blai Bonet (1926-   ), Josep Maria Espinàs (1927-   ), and Baltasar Porcel (1937-   ). With all these writers, one can speak of achievement rather than mere promise, and of all the genres it is the novel which at the moment shows the greatest variety and originality.

The situation of the post-war theatre is more precarious: though all kinds of writing have suffered from the hazards of official censorship, the difficulties of establishing a serious professional theatre in Catalan are still enormous. In these circumstances, the work of small independent groups like *A.D.B.* (*Agrupació dramàtica de Barcelona*), *E.A.D.A.G.* (*Escola d'art dramàtic Adrià Gual*), and *T.E.C.* (*Teatre experimental català*) has been immensely important.[28] All too often, however, the production of new plays has been limited to a single performance, and opportunities of seeing plays in Catalan outside Barcelona are still very restricted. Despite this, a number of interesting dramatists have emerged in the last ten or fifteen years. Several of them, like Maria Aurèlia Capmany, Manuel Pedrolo, and Baltasar Porcel, are also novelists, and to these one can add the name of Joan Brossa (1919-   ), a writer of great imagination, whose plays, like those of Pedrolo, are serious and original contributions to the theatre of the absurd.[29]

It seems appropriate, however, that the most influential play of recent years should have been Espriu's *Primera història d'Esther* (see above, p. 115), a work not originally intended for performance and conceived, in the author's words, as an epitaph for the Catalan language. As things happened, the intended obsequy became a symbol of renewal, a text which, both in its universality and in its sense of being rooted in a particular society and language, can stand for the best qualities of Catalan literature as a whole.

To sum up an entire literature is never easy, still less so when one writes as an outsider, yet Catalan literature seems to bear out as clearly as any the words of the Irish poet, W. B. Yeats:

You can no more have the greatest poetry without a nation than religion without symbols. One can only reach out to the universe with a gloved hand—that glove is one's nation, the only thing one knows even a little of.

NOTES

1. Maurici Serrahima, in his interesting article 'Sobre el Noucentisme', *SdO*, VI (1964), 7-9, describes the movement as 'the first government intervention in the history of our culture'. In fact, Prat de la Riba had a controlling interest in several of the most important intellectual bodies of the time, like the Philological Section of the *Institut d'Estudis Catalans* (established in 1911), whose original members, among them Carner, were personally chosen by him. As Albert Manent argues (op. cit., 63), the movement involves much more than literature, and is best regarded as a group of mutually dependent programmes, both cultural and political.

2. *Noucents* means 'twentieth century', but the word *noucentisme* was

probably intended to convey cultural overtones, by analogy with Italian *cinquecento*, etc.

3. J. M. Capdevila's recent study *Eugeni d'Ors, etapa barcelonina (1906-1920)* is a useful corrective to the view that Ors was the chief instigator of *noucentisme*. As we have seen, the 'new classicism' was already well established in the work of Costa i Llobera and Alcover and in the early poems of Josep Carner. In general, the dividing line between *modernisme* and *noucentisme* is less clear than many critics assume, and the main effect of the *Glosari* was to set the seal on a number of tendencies which had been gathering weight for some time.

4. 'the ilexes which burn on the smoky altar'.

5. 'Beautiful marble city of the external world, turning to gold under the gaze of love! You are made wholly with ordered care. You are purified by the blood of generous living. And, over the trivial grandeur of earth, you will hold up the palm of intelligence, which is immortal'.

6. It is clear that the death of Prat de la Riba in 1917 was a severe blow to Carner, and that he felt much less sympathetic towards Prat's successor, Cambó. The need to find a settled career in order to support a growing family must also have played a part in a decision which deprived Catalan literary life of its dominating figure.

7. 'For all things, save God, are fugitive. Who will ever describe his types of eternal brilliance in a foreign tongue and with faltering lips? Farewell, though, great clusters of punishment and avarice! To die for the new bud is pure delight! The rebel will become wholly love. For you will transcend the justice of the Father, o motherly concern for order of curds, of apples and honey!'

8. Riba's translations include two separate versions of the *Odyssey* (1919; 1948), the tragedies of Aeschylus and Sophocles, the *Lives* of Plutarch and a selection of poems by Hölderlin. His versions of Cavafy were published posthumously in 1962.

9. For a detailed discussion of some of these poems, see Arthur Terry, '*Un nu i uns ulls*: comentari a uns poemes de Carles Riba', *ER*, XI (1962), 283-303.

10. 'turned in on myself, I heard the sound of some inward sea grow nearer, far within me ripening into islands of still powerless music; a change or a birth—there was no difference: it was a sea and a sea-wind'.

11. On *Salvatge cor*, see the excellent study of Joan Ferraté, *Carles Riba, avui* (Barcelona, 1955), 31-77, and also Arthur Terry, 'Some sonnets of Carles Riba', *Hispanic studies in honour of I. González Llubera* (Oxford, 1959), 403-13.

12. 'The new excites me and I love the old'.

13. 'From real similitudes derive those of the imagination, as accidents issue from substance'.

14. See Arthur Terry, 'Sobre les *Obres poètiques* de J. V. Foix', *SdO*, X (1968), 207-12.

15. Carles Riba, *Obres completes*, II, 314-20. Critics often write as if Riba's lecture were an isolated occasion. There had, in fact, been something of a revival in the novel from 1917 onwards, though mainly at the level of popular reprints. By 1925, the influence of *noucentisme* was clearly weakening, and writers like Sagarra and Josep Pla (see above, p. 113) were showing an increasing interest in the economics of novel publishing. The two articles which Sagarra published in *La Publicitat* in the spring of 1925,

though relatively unoriginal, did have the effect of reviving a debate which was in danger of becoming sterile. Riba's lecture, which is partly a reply to Sagarra, runs counter to the general lines of the debate, to which it now seems an anachronistic postscript. The real mistake is to suppose that the interventions of Sagarra and Riba were directly responsible for a revival of novel-writing itself.

16. 'it will, therefore, take a long time for an atmosphere of humanism to surround and penetrate the body of society'.

17. On this point, see Alan Yates, '*Solitud* i els *Drames rurals*', *SdO*, XI (1969), 54-6.

18. 'Sobre la literatura catalana', *Obras completas*, V (Madrid, 1958), 672.

19. No brief survey of the *modernista* novel can do justice to its scope, as distinct from its literary quality. There were, for example, several interesting attempts to deal with the problems of the urban working classes, notably in two novels by Josep Maria Folch i Torres (1880-1950), *Aigua avall* (1907) and *Joan Endal* (1909). Folch, however, is only superficially influenced by *modernisme*, and his realism is more in the line of Oller and Galdós. *Joan Endal*, in fact, was his last novel: after 1909, he devoted himself exclusively to writing for the children's publication *En Patufet*, perhaps recognising that the social crisis which resulted in the violence of the *Semana trágica* (July 1909) demanded a more basic approach to popular education.

20. See above, p. 106 and note 15.

21. The *Normes ortogràfiques* of 1913, which now form the basis of modern Catalan spelling, were one of the greatest achievements of the grammarian Pompeu Fabra (1868-1948) and the *Institut d'Estudis Catalans*. At the time, however, they created a good deal of scandal, and helped to widen the rift between the *noucentistes* and the older writers.

22. This novel, *La gent del mas Aulet*, occupied Ruyra for almost thirty years, and shows a total inability to integrate the smaller units of his short stories into a larger whole. Its microscopic technique, though entirely in keeping with the criteria of *noucentisme*, is one of the principal reasons for its failure.

23. As a member of the Philological Section of the *Institut d'Estudis Catalans*, Ruyra collaborated with Pompeu Fabra in the preparation of the *Diccionari general de la llengua catalana* (1932), the great normative dictionary of modern Catalan.

24. For a well-documented discussion of the publishing situation and other related questions, see Francesc Vallverdú, *L'escriptor català i el problema de la llengua* (Barcelona, 1968). On the present-day status of the Catalan language, see Josep Melià, *Informe sobre la lengua catalana* (Madrid, 1970).

25. 'Pere Quart, it would appear, nowadays prefers—in poetry too—creative disorder and a painful, yet hopeful, anxiety'.

26. 'Avoid the greatest crime of all, the sin of war between brothers. Remember that in the beginning the mirror of truth was broken into tiny pieces, and that each one of these pieces nevertheless reflects an atom of true light'.

27. 'I take poetry to be a step by step description of the moral life of an ordinary man like myself ... When I write a poem, the only thing which concerns me and gives me trouble is to define as clearly as possible my moral standpoint, that is to say, the distance which separates the feeling the poem expresses from what one might call the centre of my imagination'.

28. For a useful account of the main tendencies in the post-war theatre, see Jaume Fuster, *Breu història del teatre català* (Barcelona, 1967), 88-108.

29. Since this was written, Brossa has published a large volume of poetry, *Poesia rasa* (Barcelona, 1970), containing several hundred poems written between 1943 and 1959. This book, together with his more recent collections, *Poemes civils* (1961) and *El saltamartí* (1969), establishes him beyond doubt as one of the most important poets of his generation, in a mode which owes something to Foix and the French Surrealists, but which also shows an extraordinary sensitivity to the dramatic possibilities of everyday speech.

SELECT BIBLIOGRAPHY

The following abbreviations have been used for standard series of texts: *AC* 'Antologia catalana', Edicions 62 (Barcelona); *ENC* 'Els nostres clàssics', Barcino (Barcelona).

General histories of literature and works covering particular periods

Martí de Riquer and Antoni Comas, *Història de la literatura catalana*, Ariel (Barcelona, 1964-   ), 6 vols. The three volumes so far published, by Martí de Riquer, cover the period from the early Middle Ages to the end of the seventeenth century.

Jordi Rubió i Balaguer, *Literatura catalana*, in G. Díaz-Plaja (ed.), *Historia general de las literaturas hispánicas*, Barna (Barcelona, 1949-   ), Vol. I, 643-746; Vol. III, 727-930; Vol. IV, i, 493-597; Vol. V, 213-337. Volumes III-V contain by far the most exhaustive account of the Decadence so far published.

Joaquim Molas, *Literatura catalana antiga*, Barcino (Barcelona, 1961-63), Vol. I (segle XIII); Vol. III (segle XV, i).

Josep Romeu, *Literatura catalana antiga*, Barcino (Barcelona, 1961-64), Vol. II (segle XIV); Vol. IV (segle XV, ii).

J. Ruiz i Calonja, *Història de la literatura catalana*, Teide (Barcelona, 1954).

Jordi Rubió i Balaguer, *De l'Edat Mitjana al Renaixement*, Aymà (Barcelona, 1948).

——, *La cultura catalana del Renaixement a la Decadència*, Edicions 62 (Barcelona, 1964).

(Various authors), *Un segle de vida catalana, 1814-1930*, Alcides

123

(Barcelona, 1961), 2 vols. Contains chapters on most aspects of Catalan history and culture, including literature.

Anthologies

Joan Triadú (ed.), *An anthology of Catalan lyric poetry*, Dolphin (Oxford, 1953).

J. M. Castellet and J. Molas (ed.), *Ocho siglos de poesia catalana*, Alianza (Madrid, 1970). Bilingual text.

Language and history

W. D. Elcock, *The Romance languages*, Faber (London, 1960).

P. Russell-Gebbett, *Medieval Catalan linguistic texts*, Dolphin (Oxford, 1965).

Joan Coromines, *El que s'ha de saber de la llengua catalana*, Raixa (Palma de Mallorca, 1954).

A. M. Badia i Margarit, *Llengua i cultura als països catalans*, Edicions 62 (Barcelona, 1964).

J. Vicens Vives, *Notícia de Catalunya*, Ancora (Barcelona, 1954); Spanish translation: *Noticia de Cataluña*, Destino (Barcelona, 1954).

Joan Fuster, *Nosaltres els valencians*, Edicions 62 (Barcelona, 1962).

Editions and more specialised anthologies

Chapter 1

J. Ll. Marfany (ed.), *Poesia catalana medieval*, AC (Barcelona, 1966).

Ramon Llull, *Obres essencials*, Selecta (Barcelona, 1957), 2 vols.

Arnau de Vilanova, *Obres catalanes*, ed. M. Batllori and J. Carreras Artau, *ENC* (Barcelona, 1947), 2 vols.

Jaume I, *Libre dels feyts*, ed. J. M. de Casacuberta, Barcino (Barcelona, 1926-62), 9 vols.

Bernat Desclot, *Crònica*, ed. M. Coll i Alentorn, *ENC* (Barcelona, 1949-1951), 5 vols.

Ramon Muntaner, *Crònica*, ed. J. M. de Casacuberta and M. Coll i Alentorn, Barcino (Barcelona, 1927-52), 2 vols.

Pere III, *Crònica*, ed. Amadeu J. Soberanas, Alpha (Barcelona, 1961).

Francesc Eiximenis, *Terç del Crestià*, ed. P. P. Martí de Barcelona and Norbert d'Ordal, *ENC* (Barcelona, 1929-32), 3 vols.

——, *La societat catalana al segle XIV* (anthology), ed. Jill Webster, *AC* (Barcelona, 1967).

Bernat Metge, *Obres completes*, ed. M. de Riquer, Selecta (Barcelona, 1950).

Antoni Canals, *Scipió e Anibal, De providència*, etc., ed. M. de Riquer, *ENC* (Barcelona, 1935).

J. Ll. Marfany (ed.), *Poesia catalana del segle XV, AC* (Barcelona, 1967).

Jordi de Sant Jordi, *Poesies*, ed. M. de Riquer, Universidad de Granada (Granada, 1955). Bilingual edition.

Ausias March, *Poesies*, ed. P. Bohigas, *ENC* (Barcelona, 1952-1959), 5 vols.

——, *Antologia poètica*, ed. Joan Fuster, Selecta (Barcelona, 1959). With modern Catalan versions.

Jaume Roig, *Llibre de les dones, o Spill*, ed. F. Almela i Vives, *ENC* (Barcelona, 1928).

Roiç de Corella, *Obres*, ed. R. Miquel i Planas, Biblioteca catalana (Barcelona, 1913).

Curial e Güelfa, ed. R. Aramon i Serra, *ENC* (Barcelona, 1930-1933), 3 vols.

Joanot Martorell, *Tirant lo blanc*, ed. M. de Riquer, Selecta (Barcelona, 1949).

Teatre hagiogràfic, ed. Josep Romeu, *ENC* (Barcelona, 1957), 3 vols.

Teatre profà, ed. Josep Romeu, *ENC* (Barcelona, 1962), 2 vols.

Chapter 2

E. Moreu-Rey (ed.), *El pensament il.lustrat a Catalunya, AC* (Barcelona, 1966).

Joan Ramis, *Lucrècia*, ed. J. Carbonell, *AC* (Barcelona, 1968).

Joaquim Molas (ed.), *Poesia neoclàssica i pre-romàntica*, AC (Barcelona, 1965).

Chapter 3

Joaquim Molas (ed), *Poesia catalana romàntica*, AC (Barcelona, 1965).
Jacint Verdaguer, *Obres completes*, Selecta (Barcelona, 1943).
Angel Guimerà, *Obres selectes*, Selecta (Barcelona, 1948).
Narcís Oller, *Obres completes*, Selecta (Barcelona, 1948).
——, *Memòries literaries*, Aedos (Barcelona, 1962).
Santiago Rusiñol, *Obres completes*, Selecta (Barcelona, 1947).
Joaquim Molas (ed.), *Poesia catalana de la Restauració*, AC (Barcelona, 1966).
Joan Maragall, *Obres completes*, Selecta (Barcelona, 1960-61), 2 vols.
Miquel Costa i Llobera, *Obres completes*, Selecta (Barcelona, 1947).
Joan Alcover, *Obres completes*, Selecta (Barcelona, 1964).

Chapter 4

Eugeni d'Ors ('Xènius'), *Obra catalana completa: Glosari 1906-1910*, Selecta (Barcelona, 1950).
J. M. Castellet and J. Molas (ed.), *Poesia catalana del segle XX*, Edicions 62 (Barcelona, 1963).
Joan Triadú (ed.), *Nova antologia de la poesia catalana*, Selecta (Barcelona, 1965).
José Augustin Goytisolo (ed.), *Poetas catalanes contemporáneos*, Seix Barral (Barcelona, 1968). Bilingual text.
Guerau de Liost, *Obra poètica completa, Proses literàries*, Selecta (Barcelona, 1948).
Josep Carner, *Obres completes: poesia*, Selecta (Barcelona, 1957).
Carles Riba, *Obres completes*: Vol. I (Poesia i narrativa); Vol. II (Assaigs crítics), Edicions 62 (Barcelona, 1965-67).
Joan Salvat-Papasseit, *Poesies*, Ariel (Barcelona, 1962).
J. V. Foix, *Obres poètiques*, Nauta (Barcelona, 1964).

Prudenci Bertrana, *Obres completes*, Selecta (Barcelona, 1965).

Víctor Català, *Obres completes*, Selecta (Barcelona, 1951).

Joaquim Ruyra, *Obres completes*, Selecta (Barcelona, 1949).

Llorenç Villalonga, *Obres completes I: El mite de Bearn*, Edicions 62 (Barcelona, 1966).

Xavier Berenguel, *Obres completes I*, Nauta (Barcelona, 1967).

Sebastià Juan Arbó, *Obra catalana completa I: Novel.les de l'Ebre*, Edicions 62 (Barcelona, 1966).

Josep Pla, *Obres completes*, Destino (Barcelona, 1966-   ). Twelve volumes have so far appeared.

Salvador Espriu, *Obres completes I: poesia*, Edicions 62 (Barcelona, 1968).

——, *Narracions*, AC (Barcelona, 1965).

——, *Primera història d'Esther*, AC (Barcelona, 1966).

Pere Quart (Joan Oliver), *Obra*, Fontanella (Barcelona, 1963).

Joan Oliver, *Tres comèdies*, Selecta (Barcelona, 1960).

——, *Biografia de Lot i altres proses*, Fontanella (Barcelona, 1963).

Gabriel Ferrater, *Les dones i els dies*, Edicions 62 (Barcelona, 1968).

INDEX

129